Dimensions of Multicultural Education

Dimensions of Multicultural Education

V K Jagannath

AUTHORSPRESS

Worldwide Circulation through Authorspress Global Network
First Published 2004
by Authorspress

E-35/103, Jawahar Park
Laxmi Nagar, Delhi-110 092

e-mail: authorspress@yahoo.com

Typeset in NewCenturySchlbk by Chitra Computers

Dimensions of Multicultural Education
ISBN 81-7273-127-2

Printed in India at Tarun Offset, Delhi.

Preface

We are living in a multicultural world, where many different cultures or subcultures are co-existing, with each culture being given due recognition. Now people and nations are being brought together voluntarily and involuntarily by the increasing integration of markets, the emergence of new regional political alliances, and remarkable advances in telecommunications, biotechnology and transportation that have prompted unprecedented demographic shifts. Nations around the world are faced with the problem of how to reflect the racial, ethnic, cultural and religious diversity within their societies while maintaining national unity.

To prepare citizens to function effectively in this globalised multicultural world, educational systems needs to be changed in substantial ways. Education within the pluralistic societies should affirm and help students understand their home and community cultures. It should also help free them from their cultural boundaries.

Multicultural education is an education for freedom that is essential in today's ethnically polarised and troubled world. It aims to create equal educational opportunities for students from diverse racial, ethnic, social-class, and cultural groups. It helps all students to acquire the knowledge, attitudes, and skills needed to function effectively in a pluralistic democratic society and to interact, negotiate, and communicate with peoples from diverse groups in order to create a civic and moral community that works for the common good.

The basic ideologies of multicultural education are comprehensively described in the present volume. The applications as well as challenges of multicultural curriculum are also elaborated in detail. The book will serve as a highly beneficial reference tool for policy makers, administrators, teachers and students of the globalised world.

Editor

Contents

1

Multicultural Education: Framework and Principles

Multicultural education is a field of study and an emerging discipline whose major aim is to create equal educational opportunities for students from diverse racial, ethnic, social-class, and cultural groups. Its major goal is to help all students to acquire the knowledge, attitudes, and skills needed to function effectively in a pluralistic democratic society, and to interact, negotiate, and communicate with peoples from diverse groups in order to create a civic and moral community that works for the common good. It not only draws content, concepts, paradigms, and theories from specialised interdisciplinary fields such as ethnic studies and women studies (and from history and the social and behavioural sciences). It also interrogates, challenges, and reinterprets content, concepts, and paradigms from the established disciplines.

Multicultural education as a shift in curriculum, perhaps as simple as adding new and diverse materials and perspectives to be more inclusive of traditionally under-represented groups. A multitude of differing conceptualisations of multicultural education, several shared ideals provide a basis for its understanding. While some focus on individual students or teachers, and others are much more "macro" in scope, these ideals are all, at their roots, about transformation:

i) Every student must have an equal opportunity to achieve to his full potential.

ii) Every student must be prepared to competently participate in an increasingly intercultural society.

iii) Teachers must be prepared to effectively facilitate learning for every individual student, no matter how culturally similar or different from himself.

iv) Schools must be active participants in ending oppression of all types, first by ending oppression within their own walls, then by producing socially and critically active and aware students.

v) Education must become more fully student-centred and inclusive of the voices and experiences of the students.

vi) Educators, activists, and others must take a more active role in re-examining all educational practices and how they affect the learning of all students: testing methods, teaching approaches, evaluation and assessment, school psychology and counselling, educational materials and textbooks, etc.

Components of multicultural education that are included in many educational programmes are:

i) ethnic, minority, and women's studies;

ii) bilingual programmes;

iii) cultural awareness;

iv) human relations; and

v) values clarification.

Concepts include racism, sexism, prejudice, discrimination, oppression, powerlessness, power inequality, equality, and stereotyping. If teaching a culturally diverse student population, educators need to determine the microcultures that exist in the community. One strategy for multiculturalising curriculum and instruction is teaching from a multicultural perspective. This approach will probably require some major changes in the educational programme. In this approach educators will take affirmative steps to ensure that cultural diversity and exceptionality are reflected in the curriculum. It should facilitate the development of attitudes and values conducive to the preservation and promotion of ethnic and cultural diversity as a positive quality of society. It will enhance students' self-concepts as they develop pride in their own and other cultural heritages.

Perspectives of Multicultural Education

Education that is multicultural:

i) Ensures access to learning and the resources of the education system for all students mindful of race, colour, religion, socio-economic status or gender by providing a curriculum that is responsive to their experience and knowledge and which meets their needs and interests.

ii) Provides a framework for all students to examine and appreciate their own cultural backgrounds, how cultures operate, and the roles individuals and groups play in the creation and interpretation of culture.

iii) Promotes cross-cultural awareness in all students and interaction through experiences that enhance understanding and respect for the languages and heritages of others and encourage the use of cultural diversity as a resource.

iv) Develops in all students the skills, knowledge, values and attitudes to participate as active and informed citizens.

The multicultural perspective applies to the whole curriculum. It influences outcomes, content, learning and teaching strategies, and assessment, reporting and evaluation in all key learning areas. Schools cannot avoid transmitting values and cannot operate independently of the predominant culture. Through implementing a multicultural perspective, students, teachers, schools and systems share cultures and explore constructions of ethnicity, race, gender and class. They can reflect critically on the role education and other social structures play in the perpetuation of dominant cultural values and power relationships.

The concept of culture is complex and dynamic. Culture encompasses the meanings and values that evolve among groups of people over time, influenced by and responding to a complex range of experiences, relationships and conditions of life. Culture is expressed through such things as language, gesture and stance, customs, history, religion, law, architecture, symbols, sex roles, power relationships, property rights, music, art, literature, dance, food and drink, sport, technology, communications, marriage rules, social and family structures, rituals, celebrations, myths, superstitions, rules of hygiene, and entertainment. In this complex environment cultural identity develops.

Factors such as age, gender, class, ethnicity and sexuality contribute to its evolution. They are also factors in the emergence of diversity within cultures. The interplay of these influences contributes to change within cultures. Culture is not a static collection of traditions, beliefs and practices. This notion reinforces misconceptions and stereotypes. Culture is essentially dynamic, responding to and incorporating changed circumstances and new influences.

Individuals live in and between many different cultures and identities—in their work, school, family and social lives. While cultures have things in common, differing life experiences and perceptions result in individuals and groups developing a range of cultural understandings and behaviours. The challenge for multicultural education is to provide students with opportunity to share cultures, to look below their surface features to deeper levels of shared meaning. Even though people outside a culture rarely understand cultural meanings completely, through a multicultural education students will gain in awareness and appreciation of their own and other cultures.

All students need to develop a multicultural perspective in order to enhance:

i) A good self-concept and self-understanding.

ii) Sensitivity to and understanding of others.

iii) The ability to perceive and understand multiple, sometimes conflicting, cultural and national interpretations of and perspectives on events, values, and behaviour.

iv) The ability to make decisions and take effective action based on a multicultural analysis and synthesis.

v) Open minds when addressing issues.

vi) Understanding of the process of stereotyping, a low degree of stereotypical thinking, and pride in self and respect for all peoples.

Evolution of Multicultural Education

The historical roots of multicultural education lie in the civil rights movements of various historically oppressed groups. Many trace the history of multicultural education back to the social action of African Americans and other people of colour who challenged discriminatory practices in public institutions during the civil rights struggles of the 1960s. Among those institutions specifically targeted were educational institutions, which were among the most oppressive and hostile to the ideals of racial equality. Activists, community leaders, and parents called for curricular reform and insisted on a re-examination of hiring practices.

In the early 1970s, the women's rights movement joined this push for education reform. Women's rights groups challenged inequities in employment and educational opportunities as well as income, identifying education as a primary contributing factor in institutionalised and systemic sexism. Feminist scholars and other women activists, like groups of colour before them, insisted on curricula more inclusive of their histories and experiences. They challenged the discrepancy low number of female administrators relative to the percentage of female teachers.

Sensing progress by groups of colour and women in their struggles for human rights and social and educational change into the early 1970s, other traditionally oppressed groups found growing support and energy for their movements. Through the 1970s, gay and lesbian groups, the elderly, and people with disabilities organised visible and powerful pushes for sociopolitical and human rights. As schools, universities, and other educational institutions and organisations scrambled to address the concerns of these and other historically marginalised groups, a host of programmes, practices, and policies emerged, mostly focused on slight changes or additions to traditional curriculum.

Together, the separate actions of these various groups who were dissatisfied with the inequities of the education system, along with the resulting reaction of educational institutions during the late 1960s and 1970s, defined the earliest conceptualisation of multicultural education. The 1980s saw the emergence of a body of scholarship on multicultural education by progressive education activists and researchers who refused to allow schools to address their concerns by simply adding token programmes and special units on famous women or famous people of colour.

James Banks, one of the pioneers of multicultural education, was among the first multicultural education scholars to examine schools as social systems from a multicultural context. He grounded his conceptualisation of multicultural education in the idea of "educational equality". According to Banks, in order to maintain a "multicultural school environment", all aspects of the school had to be examined and transformed, including policies, teachers' attitudes, instructional materials, assessment methods, counselling, and teaching styles.

By the late 1980s, other K-12 teachers-turned-scholars including Carl Grant, Christine Sleeter, Geneva Gay, and Sonia Nieto provided more scholarship in multicultural education, developing new, deeper frameworks that were grounded in the ideal of equal educational opportunity and a connection between school transformation and social change. In order to move beyond slight curricular changes, which many argued only further differentiated between the curricular "norm" and the marginalised "other", they built on Banks's work, examining other structural foundations of schools and how these contributed to educational inequities.

Tracking, culturally oppressive teaching approaches, standardised tests, school funding discrepancies, classroom climate, discriminatory hiring practices, and other symptoms of an ailing and oppressive education system were exposed, discussed, and criticised. Meanwhile, the cultural landscape of the United States continued to become less visibly white Christian and more visibly rich with cultural, racial, ethnic, and religious diversity, underscoring the necessity for everyone to develop a set of skills and knowledge that the present system was failing to provide all students. These included creative and critical thinking skills, intercultural competence, and social and global awareness. The education system was not only plagued by unequal treatment of traditionally oppressed groups, but was also ill-equipped to prepare even the most highly privileged students to competently participate in an increasingly diverse society.

In the 1990s, multicultural education scholars refocused the struggle on developing new approaches and models of education and learning built on a foundation of social justice, critical thinking, and equal opportunity. Educators, researchers, and cultural theorists began to further deconstruct traditional models in both the K-12 and higher education arenas from a multicultural framework.

Joel Spring, Peter McLaren, Henry Giroux, and others contributed to a new body of critical sociocultural criticism of educational institutions within the context of larger societal and global dimensions of power, privilege, and economics, and the intersections of these. What started as small curricular shifts and additions has become a framework for re-examining both schools and society from a progressive and transformative framework. As long as we continue to operate within the existing capitalist social relations of the larger society, there is good reason to believe that racism and social injustice will continue to pose a serious threat to democracy and that the dream of social equality will remain largely unrealised. So, while work continues toward school transformation, the emerging conceptualisations of multicultural education stress that this work must be understood relative to the social and political structures that currently control education in the United States, and that the two are intrinsically linked.

Multicultural education, in its determination to address the ills and shortcomings of the current education system, can be a starting point to eliminating inequities in society. Today, literally dozens of models and frameworks for multicultural education exist. While theory and scholarship has moved from small curricular revisions to approaches that call for full transformations of self, schools, and society, many implementations of multicultural education still begin with curricular additions of diverse sources. But with a fuller understanding of the roots of the movement, we are better equipped to follow the transformative path laid by many educators, activists, and scholars.

Approaches to Multicultural Education

In his book *Multicultural Education as Social Activism*, C.E. Sleeter delineates five approaches to multicultural education:

i) Advocates of the *Teaching the Culturally Different Approach* attempt to raise the academic achievement of students of colour through culturally relevant instruction.

ii) In the *Human Relations Approach* students are taught about commonalties of all people through understanding their social and cultural differences but not their differences in institutional and economic power.

iii) The *Single Group Studies Approach* is about the histories and contemporary issues of oppression of people of colour, women, low socio-economic groups, and gays and lesbians.

iv) The *Multicultural Education Approach* promotes the transformation of the educational process to reflect the ideals of democracy in a pluralistic society. Students are taught content using instructional methods that value cultural knowledge and differences.

v) Educators who use the *Social Reconstructionist Approach* to multicultural education go a step further to teach students about oppression and discrimination. Students learn about their roles as social change agents so that they may participate in the generation of a more equitable society.

These categories overlap, and educators may use more than one approach simultaneously.

In view of an increasingly multicultural society and student population, multicultural educators reflect the need to address the systemic, curricular, and pedagogical impediments to the learning of traditionally marginalised students. Multicultural educators also recognise that a increasingly multicultural nation and a shrinking and contentious planet at the edge of the twenty-first century demands a people who are critical thinkers and able to deal with the complexities of multicultural differences.

The practice of multicultural education in the schools is often criticised for trivialising the goal of multicultural education, which is the transformation of schooling to include the needs and perspectives of many cultures in shaping the ways in which children are educated and thus, the transformation of society.

Multicultural education requires critical thinking with attention paid to complexity. It requires research and learning about the multiple perspectives involved in any historical or contemporary experience in order to understand the rich meaning therein.

Multicultural education is often given narrow parameters. Many think of it as education only for students of colour. Certainly there is a substantial need for the education of ethnic minorities. Racism has created an educational system which continues to ignore the culture of students of colour in learning and tracks many of them into continued subordinate positions in society. A restructuring of schools to meet their needs is essential. However, children of colour do not live in a vacuum. In a democratic, multicultural society all children must be educated about the multiple strands of the past that have created the webs of the present.

Multicultural education also provides a perspective for mathematics and science. Ethno-mathematics presents a view of mathematical thinking that incorporates the ways in which culture and mathematics are intertwined. Mathematics is an aspect of all cultures. In the sciences there is the opportunity to study environments from the perspectives of the diversity of cultural knowledge, to approach non-western science as legitimate knowledge construction, or to include social justice as an aspect of science.

Dimension of Multicultural Education

J. A. Banks describes the dimensions of multicultural education in five overlapping areas in which researchers and practitioners are involved.

i) *Content integration* is the inclusion of materials, concepts, and values from a variety of cultures in teaching.
ii) *Knowledge construction* is the recognition that all knowledge is socially constructed, created in the minds of human beings to explain their experience and thus, can be challenged. Ideas that shape society do change. As such, knowledge construction is a primary aspect of multicultural education because before teachers can effectively teach multiculturally they must reconstruct their world views.

iii) *Equity pedagogy* is involved when teachers alter their teaching methods to accommodate the various cultural differences of diverse students to stimulate academic achievement.

iv) *Prejudice reduction* concerns changing the students' attitudes towards differences of race and ethnicity. Prejudice reduction can also include teaching tolerance about religion, physical and mental abilities, and sexual preference.

v) An empowering school culture is the dimension of multicultural education that enables the other four dimensions.

Educators must examine the structures of education that impede learning and empower students and families from diverse racial, ethnic, and gender groups. The aim is to create schools that encourage the full development of all students.

Focus of Multicultural Education

Multicultural education must have, as its crux, the below defining characteristics to achieve its purposes for students, teachers, parents, and administrators of the school system:

a) a learning environment that supports positive interracial contact;

b) a multicultural curriculum;

c) positive teacher expectations;

d) administrative support; and,

e) teacher training workshops.

If one of the features is absent, frustration and heightened resentment may occur as backlash behaviours multiply.

The effects of a positive multicultural climate may manifest in a number of ways, such as:

a) diminished pockets of segregation among student body;
b) less racial tension in the schools;
c) increased ethnic minority retention and classroom performance; and,
d) inclusion of a multicultural curriculum.

The multicultural educational environment should not be a microcosm of our present society, with regard to issues of diversity and tolerance. Many factors determine a successful multicultural atmosphere, but the features as outlined above may be important indications of success.

Administrative support for multicultural education is critical. How can a house stand if the foundation is fragile. Multicultural education will be as successful as commitment to it by school administrators. Regardless of the level of commitment (local, state, and/or national), programmes initiated under the guise of multiculturalism must receive reinforcement from administrators who are accountable for the success of established multicultural initiatives. A key factor in any proposed multicultural initiative is curriculum development.

A multicultural curriculum should be considered for several reasons:

a) provides alternative points of view relative to information already taught in most educational systems;
b) provides ethnic minorities with a sense of being inclusive in history, science etc.; and,
c) decreases stereotypes, prejudice, bigotry, and racism.

Principles of Teaching and Learning

Cultural diversity in schools is both an opportunity and a challenge. In this era of intertnationalistaion nations are becoming enriched by the ethnic, cultural, and language diversity among their citizens and within schools. However, whenever diverse groups interact, intergroup tension, stereotypes, and institutionalised discrimination develop. Schools must find ways to respect the diversity of their students as well as help to create a unified nation to which all citizens have allegiance.

To help educational policy makers and practitioners to realise the elusive and difficult but essential goal of a democratic and pluralistic society, several principles and frameworks have been proposed by scholars and educational research centres. The principles designed by the Multicultural Education Consensus Panel, USA, is found to be much beneficial. The Panel sponsored by the Centre for Multicultural Education at the University of Washington and the Common Destiny Alliance at the University of Maryland reviewed and synthesised research related to diversity during a four-year period. The findings of the Panel, which are called essential principles, describe ways in which educational policy and practice related to diversity can be improved. These principles are derived from research and practice. They are designed to help educational practitioners in all types of schools increase student academic achievement and improve intergroup skills. Each of the essential principles are summarised below.

Teacher Learning

Principle 1: Professional development programmes should help teachers understand the complex characteristics of ethnic groups within US society and the ways in which race, ethnicity, language, and social class interact to influence student behaviour.

Student Learning

Principle 2: Schools should ensure that all students have equitable opportunities to learn and to meet high standards.

Principle 3: The curriculum should help students understand that knowledge is socially constructed and reflects researchers personal experiences as well as the social, political, and economic contexts in which they live and work.

Principle 4: Schools should provide all students with opportunities to participate in extra- and co-curricular activities that develop knowledge, skills, and attitudes that increase academic achievement and foster positive interracial relationships.

Intergroup Relations

Principle 5: Schools should create or make salient superordinate crosscutting group memberships in order to improve intergroup relations.

Principle 6: Students should learn about stereotyping and other related biases that have negative effects on racial and ethnic relations.

Principle 7: Students should learn about the values shared by virtually all cultural groups (e.g., justice, equality, freedom, peace, compassion, and charity).

Principle 8: Teachers should help students acquire the social skills needed to interact effectively with students from other racial, ethnic, cultural, and language groups.

Principle 9: Schools should provide opportunities for students from different racial, ethnic, cultural, and language groups to interact socially under conditions designed to reduce fear and anxiety.

School Governance, Organisation and Equity

Principle 10: A schools organisational strategies should ensure that decision making is widely shared and that members of the school community learn collaborative skills and dispositions in order to create a caring environment for students.

Principle 11: Leaders should develop strategies that ensure that all public schools, regardless of their locations, are funded equitably.

Assessment

Principle 12: Teachers should use multiple culturally sensitive techniques to assess complex cognitive and social skills.

References

Bennett, C., *Comprehensive multicultural education: Theory and Practice,* Massachusetts: Allen & Bacon, 1995.

Banks, J. A., *Diversity within Unity: Essential Principles for Teaching and Learning in a Multicultural Society*, CME Publications, University of Washington, Seattle, 1995.

_____________ *Education in the 80s: Multiethnic education,* Washington, D.C.: National Education Association, 1981

_____________ , *Teaching Strategies for Ethnic Studies*, Boston: Allyn and Bacon, 1997.

_____________ , C. A. M. Banks (eds.), *Multicultural Education: Issues and Perspectives,* Boston: Allyn and Bacon, 1997.

Glazer, N., *We Are All Multiculturalists Now*, Cambridge, MA: Harvard University Press, 1997.

Gloria Ladson Billings, *New Directions in Multicultural Education: Complexities, Boundaries, and Critical Race Theory,* University of Wisconsin, Madison.

Gordon, B. M., "Knowledge Construction, Competing Critical Theories, and Education", In *Handbook of Research on Multicultural Education*, J. A. Banks and C. A. McGee Banks (eds.), New York: Macmillan, 1995

Gollnick, D. M., Chinn, P. C., *Multicultural Education in a Pluralistic Society,* St. Louis: Mosby, 1990.

Irvine, J. J., and York, D. E., "Learning Styles and Culturally Diverse Students". In *Handbook of Research on Multicultural Education*, edited by J. A. Banks and C. A. McGee Banks, New York: Macmillan, 1995.

Lynch, James, *Education for Citizenship in a multicultural society*, London/New York, Cassell, 1992.

Nieto, S. , "School reform and student Achievement: A multicultural perspective", in J. A. Banks, C. A. M. Banks (eds.), *Multicultural Education: Issues and Perspectives,* Boston: Allyn and Bacon, 1997.

Olneck, M., "The recurring dream: Symbolism and ideology in intercultural and multicultural education", *American Journal of Education,* 98(2), 147–174, 1990.

Sleeter, C. E. , *Multicultural Education as Social Activism*, Albany: State University of New York Press, 1997.

Willett, C. (ed.), *Theorising Multiculturalism: A Guide to the Current Debate*, Malden, MA: Blackwell, 1998.

2

Transformation of Meaningful Classroom

The increasing recognition that children have and should develop multiple ways of "seeing" and "knowing" has provided an impetus for schools to expand the curriculum beyond the teaching of logical/mathematical, and verbal knowledge to include the "multiple intelligences" that make up the classroom. In a developmentally appropriate classroom, the development of "aesthetic literacy" is encouraged through the exploration of poetry, dance, painting, and music. In addition, the appreciation of multiple and diverse ways of seeing and "making sense" of the world is encouraged through the recognition and celebration of multicultural diversity.

Multicultural education is seen as a perspective that should be integrated throughout all subject areas. Not only does such a curriculum help all children to develop cultural sensitivity and understanding, but it helps children from culturally diverse backgrounds connect the unfamiliar (the school culture) with the familiar (the home culture). Bowman describes culture as a prism created from shared meaning; members of a cultural group see the world from a different perspective, making sense of their experience in different ways. The absence of continuity and congruence between the child's home culture and the school—an absence of shared meaning—may interfere with children's competent functioning in the new setting.

In a developmentally appropriate classroom, learning involves the "whole child" and addresses all four components of learning identified: knowledge, skills, dispositions, and feelings. The curriculum strives to help children become lifelong learners, who can think critically and imaginatively, ask meaningful questions and formulate alternative solutions, appreciate diversity, work collaboratively, and perhaps most importantly, have the capacity to form caring relationships with others.

Creating a Multicultural School Environment

Educators around the world are increasingly called upon to solve problems stemming from different and sometimes conflicting interests of ethnically, culturally, and socially distinct populations. Essential to living and working in increasingly culturally diverse schools, workplaces, and communities, is a perspective that cultural diversity is not a problem or crisis but rather an incredibly exciting opportunity enabling us to experience other peoples and cultures. In one sense, multicultural education is an argument for an 'indigenisation' of the schools so that educational programmes might more truly represent the cultural and political interests of the particular children and communities involved. In another sense, it is an argument for the importance of all children receiving the advantages of cross-cultural experience that gives them meaningful skills as well as values, facilitating their participation in cross-cultural collaboration.

The following are the components for creating multicultural school environment:

i) Active involvement of the school community
ii) School policy
iii) Redistribution of power and authority within school and classrooms
iv) High expectations by teachers
v) Curriculum issues that involve infusion, language study, individual learning style and personnel.

Active involvement of the school community, is a necessary component of creating multicultral shcool environment.

Taking a lesson from higher education where cultural diversity has been given more attention, "Cultural diversity programmes have been successful on campuses where faculty have been actively involved in changing the campus environment." As in the development of a comprehensive alcohol and drug prevention effort, this means the establishment of a multicultural task force that consists of youth, teachers, the principal, other school personnel, parents, and community representatives.

Another essential component is the collaborative development embraces the philosophy that the school is committed to all students receiving an education that continuously affirms human diversity, that validates the history and culture of all ethnic groups, that is based on high expectations for academic success for all students, and that encourages students' active participation in the school. Therefore, in a school with a large number of black students, for example, all other cultures — Hispanic, Asian, Native American, Jewish, White, etc.,— are valued. In other words, the racial/ethnic composition of the school is independent of its mission and implementing curriculum.

The third component in developing a culturally transformed school is the redistribution of power and authority within the school and classroom. Since the school is a microcosm of the larger society in which ethnic minorities, and youth have systemically been denied access to power, moving toward multiculturalism necessitates empowering ethnic minority children.

Critical to a restructuring effort which redistributes power in the classroom and school is the establishment of cooperative learning and other peer rescurce programmes in which all youth and teachers are given opportunities to be leaders and to help others. Effectively redistributing power and restructuring the schools and classrooms and, thus, building multiculturalism, also necessitates dealing directly with the issue of power. The cultural sensitivity training process allows individuals to develop sensitivity to cultural identity and to the dynamics of power and powerlessness which profoundly affect the educational process.

A fourth essential component in establishing a school environment that celebrates diversity is closely related to the power issue: high expectations by teachers for ethnic minority children and youth. Perhaps no point has been reiterated in all the school effectiveness literature as much as this one.

Curriculum is the last component for effective multicultural programming. As classrooms become more and more culturally diverse, the need to infuse multicultural content into the curriculum becomes increasingly evident.

Integrating multicultural content into the curriculum involves four approaches:

i) *Contributions approach* focuses on heroes, holidays, and discrete elements and is the most extensively used approach to multiculturalism in the schools. In this approach, the traditional ethnocentric curriculum remains unchanged in its basic structure, goals, and salient characteristics. Cultural traditions, foods, music, and dance may be discussed, but little or no attention is given to their meaning and significance to minority groups.

ii) *Additive approach* adds content, concepts, themes, and perspectives of minority groups to the curriculum without changing its structure. For instance, teachers may add a book, unit, or course to the curriculum that focuses on diverse groups or topics. However, the students may not have the knowledge base to understand multicultural concepts, issues, and groups.

iii) *Transformational approach* involves changing the structure of the curriculum to enable students to view concepts, issues, events, and themes from the perspectives of minority groups.

iv) *In social action approach* students make decisions on important social issues and take action to help solve them. Students feel empowered and are proactive; they are provided with the knowledge, values, and skills necessary to participate in social change. Student self-examination becomes central in this approach through value analysis, decision making, problem solving, and social action experiences.

While social studies is a prime subject matter area in which to infuse such content, the common misconception exists that a "multicultural curriculum" only is relevant to social studies. Multiculturalism necessitates including in social studies a global education approach which includes the study of human values, global systems, global problems and issues, and the history of contacts and interdependence among peoples, cultures, and nations. The study of culture is the study of the richness of ways in which human beings solve the issues of life as an individual, group member, and integral systemic component of spaceship earth: academics, vocations, arts, and human relationships.

The study of cultures provides is the opportunity for students to learn an anthropological approach to viewing their society and world; that is, they would learn "to describe before they prescribe"; to listen without bias; to learn the difference between the usually confused concepts of culture, race and class; and to develop the critical thinking skills that are necessary to becoming a productive person in the future workforce. The study of culture would be greatly facilitated by an interdisciplinary, theme-focused curriculum instead of a fragmented subject-based one. An important issue in working toward multiculturalism is that of language. It is essential to value the primary language of language-minority children, even giving them language credit for this facility, encouraging them to develop their primary language skills, and allowing them to speak their primary language except when English is the focus of instruction.

The four issues—infusion, language study, individual learning style, and personnel needs—are the key to creating a multiculturally sensitive school. Numerous specific strategies exist that are also basic to successful prevention programming for all youth and especially for ethnic minority youth, strategies that are topics of study in their own right: reduced class size; home-school collaboration; middle school reform; culturally sensitive assessment tools; buddy systems; peer resource programmes; student support groups; rap groups; mentoring programmes; international exchange programmes; school-to-work transition programmes; school-based social and health services; youth service; career education; after-school; student cultural organisations; cross-district integration programmes such as magnet schools; etc. However, many of these strategies will flow naturally once you have a school that has bought into a multiculturalism perspective.

Proponents of an integrated curriculum strive to create such a classroom environment by encouraging active, engaged learning, through open-ended discussion and multiple modes of inquiry. Based on brain research, which demonstrates that the mind is designed to perceive patterns and relationships and works best when learning takes place in the context of meaningful activities, integrated curricular approaches encourage children to bring all of their intelligences and experience to the learning activity.

Teachers act as coach, facilitator, and partner in inquiry, suggesting and providing resources and strategies. Subjects, rather than being separated into discrete areas, each with its own sequence of skills, are integrated. It is important to note that an integrated curriculum is not synonymous with fuzzy-mindedness.

Curriculum, then, becomes a negotiation, a balance achieved among three sources of input: children's interests, teachers' interests, and the required unit. Learning is characterised by a joint search for understanding, with teachers and children becoming partners in inquiry. The key to realising the full potential of this process is the teacher's ability to facilitate sharing in a way that is naturally respectful of the children's ideas. This single element may be the most elusive and difficult aspect of an inquiry curriculum.

Learning centres provide opportunities for children to learn through concrete experiences with materials and other children. A typical preschool and kindergarten classroom may be divided into a number of such centres, including housekeeping or dramatic play; a block corner; sand and water; art; reading; writing; and a science centre. A thematic curriculum can help provide structure for children's independent and collaborative explorations and activities. Although learning centres are usually not used in older elementary classrooms, older children may benefit from hands-on learning opportunities which engage all the senses.

TRANSFORMATION OF MULTICULTURAL CURRICULUM

As a a progressive approach for transforming education that holistically critiques and addresses current shortcomings, failings, and discriminatory practices in education, multicultural education is grounded in ideals of social justice, education equity, and a dedication to facilitating educational experiences in which all students reach their full potential as learners and as socially aware and active beings, locally, nationally, and globally. It acknowledges that schools are essential to laying the foundation for the transformation of society and the elimination of oppression and injustice. The underlying goal of multicultural education is to affect social change. The pathway toward this goal incorporates three strands of transformation:

i) the transformation of self;
ii) the transformation of schools and schooling:
iii) the transformation of society.

Transforming of self: Multicultural education must be a process through which all aspects of education are examined and critiqued, and rebuilt on ideals of equity and social justice. Most people who identify with multicultural education as an important process for improving education for all students agree that transformation—large scale change—is needed in curriculum, pedagogy, assessment, and other aspects of schools and schooling. A majority of multicultural education courses and workshops focus on these pieces of the education puzzle. Most multicultural educators would also agree that some level of self-reflection and self-critique are important. But even those who are willing to fully engage in a discussion about curriculum transformation are often resistant to a discussion about self-change, or self-transformation, at the same level or depth.

Transformation of school : Multicultural education calls for a critical examination of all aspects of schooling. Aspects of multicultural school transformation include the following:

i) *Student-centered pedagogy*

a) The experiences of students must be brought to the fore in the classroom, making learning more active, interactive, and engaging.

b) Traditional teaching approaches and pedagogical models must be deconstructed to examine how they are contributing to and supporting institutional systems of oppression.

c) Known oppressive practices like tracking (even if informal) must be exposed and critically examined.

d) All aspects of teaching and learning in schools must be refocused on, and rededicated to, the students themselves instead of standardised test scores and school rankings.

e) Emphasis should be put on critical and creative thinking, learning skills, and deep social awareness as well as facts and figures.

f) Pedagogy must provide all students with equal potential to reach their potential as learners.

g) Pedagogy must be flexible enough to allow for the diversity of learning styles present in every classroom.

ii) *Multicultural curriculum*

a) All curricula must be studied for accuracy and completeness.

b) All subjects must be told from diverse perspectives—this is related to accuracy and completeness.

c) "Inclusive curriculum" also means including the voices of the students in the classroom.

d) Curricula should reflect the diversity of learning styles in every classroom.

iii) *Inclusive educational media and materials*

a) Educational materials should be inclusive of diverse voices and perspectives.

b) Students must be encouraged to think critically about materials and media.

iv) *Supportive school and classroom climate*

a) Teachers must be better prepared to foster a positive classroom climate for all students.

b) Overall school cultures must be closely examined to determine how they might be cycling and supporting oppressive societal conditions.

c) Administrative hierarchies in schools must be examined to assess whether they produce positive teaching environments for all teachers.

d) Teachers and administrators must be held accountable for practices deemed to be racist, sexist, heterosexist, classist, or in any other way discriminatory.

v) *Continual evaluation and assessment*

a) Educators and education researchers must continue to examine the emphasis on standardised test scores and develop more just alternatives for measuring student "achievement", "ability", or "potential".

b) Continuing evaluation measures must be taken to measure the success of new and existing programmes meant to provide more opportunities to groups traditionally and presently underrepresented in colleges and universities.

Transformation of society: The ultimate goal of multicultural education is to contribute progressively and proactively to the transformation of society and to the application and maintenance of social justice and equity. This stands to reason, as the transformation of schools necessarily transforms a society that puts so much stock in educational attainment, degrees, and test scores. In fact, it is particularly this competitive, capitalistic framing of the dominant mentality of the United States that multicultural education aims to challenge, shake, expose, and critique.

This is precisely the reason that it is not enough to continue working within an ailing, oppressive, and outdated system to make changes, when the problems in education are themselves symptoms of a system that continues to be controlled by the economic elite. One does not need to study education too closely to recognise that schools consistently provide continuing privilege to the privileged and continuing struggle for the struggling with very little hope of upward mobility. "Informal" tracking, standardised testing, discrepancies in the quality of schools within and across regions, and other practices remain from the industrial-age model of schools. Only the terminology has changed—and the practices are not quite as overt.

Educators, educational theorists, researchers, activists, and everyone else must continue to practice and apply multicultural teaching and learning principles both inside and out of the classroom. In a sense, multicultural education uses the transformation of self and school as a metaphor and starting place for the transformation of society. Ultimately, social justice and equity in schools can, and should, mean social justice and equity in society. Only then will the purpose of multicultural education be fully achieved.

Stages of Curriculum Transformation

Just as there are several conceptualisations for multicultural education, there are several perceptions as to what constitutes multicultural curriculum transformation. Approaches for multicultural curriculum transformation range from slight curricular changes to a fully-revised social awareness and action conceptualisations. James Banks, Peggy McIntosh and others have formulated continuums for curricular reform that help move transformation efforts from the former toward the latter.

The following stages of curriculum transformation have been adapted from several existing models including those by Banks and McIntosh.

Stage 1: Curriculum of the Mainstream

The curriculum of the mainstream is Eurocentric and male-centric. It fully ignores the experiences, voices, contributions, and perspectives of non-dominant individuals and groups in all subject areas. All educational materials including textbooks, films, and other teaching and learning tools present information in a purely Eurocentric, male-centric format. This stage is harmful for both students who identify with mainstream culture as well as individuals from non-dominant groups. It has negative consequences for the former because, according to Banks it:

> reinforces their false sense of superiority, gives them a misleading conception of their relationship with other racial and ethnic groups, and denies them the opportunity to benefit from the knowledge, perspectives, and frames of reference that can be gained from studying and experiencing other cultures and groups.

The curriculum of the mainstream has negative consequences for students from non-dominant groups by failing to validate their culture, experiences, and perspectives. According to Banks, it further alienates students who already struggle to survive in a school culture that differs so greatly from their home cultures.

Stage 2: Heroes and Holidays

Teachers at this stage "celebrate" difference by integrating information or resources about famous people and the cultural artifacts of various groups into the mainstream curriculum. Bulletin boards may contain pictures of Martin Luther King, Jr. or W.E.B. DuBois, and teachers may plan special celebrations for Black History Month or Women's History Month. Learning about "other cultures" focuses on costumes, foods, music, and other tangible cultural items.

The strengths of this stage are that the teacher is attempting to diversify the curriculum by providing materials and knowledge outside the mainstream culture and that the Heroes and Holidays approach is fairly easy to implement with little new knowledge needed by the teacher. Still, the weaknesses heavily outweigh the strengths:

— By focusing celebratory attention on non-dominant groups outside the context of the rest of the curriculum, the teacher is further defining these groups as "the other".

— Curricula at this stage fail to address the real experiences of non-dominant groups instead focusing on the accomplishments of a few heroic characters. Students may learn to consider the struggles of non-dominant groups as "extra" information instead of important knowledge in their overall understanding of the world.
— The special celebrations at this stage are often used for justification—not to truly transform the curriculum.

The Heroes and Holidays approach trivialises the overall experiences, contributions, struggles, and voices of non-dominant groups, fitting directly into a Eurocentric, male-centric curriculum.

Stage 3: Integration

At the integration stage, teachers move beyond heroes and holidays to add substantial materials and knowledge about non-dominant groups to the curriculum. The teacher may add to her or his collection of books those by authors of colour or by women.

The strengths of the intergration stage are that it moves beyond special celebrations to deal with real issues and concepts and that it more closely ties the new material into the rest of the curriculum. But many weaknesses remain:

— New materials and units become secondary resources and knowledge as textbooks and the meat of the curriculum are still based on a Eurocentric, male-centric orientation.
— New information is still delivered from a Eurocentric, male-centric perspective.

Stage 4: Structural Reform

New materials, perspectives, and voices are woven seamlessly with current frameworks of knowledge to provide new levels of understanding from a more complete and accurate curriculum. The teacher dedicates herself or himself to continuously expanding her or his knowledge base through the exploration of various sources from various perspectives, and sharing that knowledge with her or his students. Students learn to view events, concepts, and facts through various lenses.

Stage 5: Multicultural, Social Action and Awareness

In addition to the changes made in the structural reform stage, important social issues including racism, sexism, and classism are directly addressed in the curriculum. The voices, ideas, and perspectives of the students regarding these and all other topics are brought to the fore in the learning experience — the students themselves becoming yet another multicultural classroom resource. The textbook is viewed as a single perspective among many, and the relevance of its limitations, along with those of other educational media, are explored and discussed.

Characteristics of Culturally Meaningful Schools

Traditionally, our school system was designed for history's definition of who ought to be educated. The belief was that not all children required an education. Throughout the history, there have always been jobs on the farms or in the factories, making a high dropout rate acceptable. Thus, schools that only worked for some children and not for all children have been accepted as normal from the very beginning. Today as our society is changing, our demographics are changing, and so, too, must our educational beliefs and practices change. It is from this realisation that the impetus comes to create schools that work for all children. A school that works for all children must be grounded in a value system of cooperation and relationships. This means that real school reform requires a transforming from the historical core values upon which our public schools are based into an ethic that puts 'us' first and 'I' second. It means schools reflecting the following characteristics:

Effective Leadership

We all know intuitively and the effective schools research shows us empirically, that quality schools require quality principals. But in addition to an inspired, entrepreneurial principal schools need leadership — both formal and informal — that is shared among staff, parents, students, and community. Quality schools require a shared responsibility serving in leadership roles. They may rotate, change from person to person, group to group, or they may not. But these schools know that the kind of leadership that counts, that makes a difference, is the leadership that comes from the schools themselves, not from the top of a school district's hierarchy.

Unity of Purpose

Schools must have a purpose and a vision of where they are going. This includes a clearly articulated set of core values that serve as the underpinnings for the decisions made on behalf of the children. What is critical is that this purpose, this vision, and this set of core values is known and shared by all of the adults and children in the school. This means that a shared decision-making process helped create them, shared leadership helps keep them visible and present to all, and that decisions made in the school consciously reflect these values.

A major role of school leaders is to keep the purpose of the school visible tangible and alive for everyone. Leaders must find the real and symbolic ways to keep the mission vital and present on a daily basis in their writings words and daily actions. Leaders must help keep the dream alive day in and day out.

Pervasive Caring and Nurturing School Environment

If we are going to change the dominant cultural value system from competition and rugged individualism to cooperation and relationship it means that we must put forth the behaviour that recognises that human beings need warmth, love, affection and affirmation. And that children learn and thrive in that nurturing kind of an environment.

Schools have not seen it as important, historically, to be environments of pervasive caring and nurturing. We see a great deal of blame placed upon children. We often hear the argument put forth, even in kindergarten, that life is tough so we must toughen up the children. The truth is, children do better in safe and nurturing environments. Children do not do as well in environments where adults are continually critical, constantly accentuating the negative, and not accepting children for who they are. Since we know this is true, then we are obligated to foster warm and caring environments where children will blossom.

All Adults are Responsible for All Children

Due to the dramatic and alarming changes in our demographics and in our families, our villages now include schools, teachers, assistants, neighbours, the business community, and an ever expanding list of concerned citizens. All of us have a stake in the success of our children. The pronouns must change to "we" and "our". Teachers, by and large, have been trained in colleges of education to think about "their" students in "their" classrooms almost to the exclusion of the rest of the school.

Teachers have been so focused on what happens within their own four walls that there is little interest in, or time for, the school as a whole unless of course, some decision or event directly effects them and/or their students. This long standing and deeply entrenched practice occurs in so many ways in our schools every day. For example, during lunch period at a typical urban elementary school, two teachers have just finished eating and have decided to take a little walk before class starts. They have ten minutes left in their 30 minute duty free lunch. As they walk down the hallway they notice a group of students engaged in noisy and obviously inappropriate behaviour. The first thought the teachers have is "Are those my students?" If any one or all of the students happens to be in their classrooms, the teachers, without question, will intervene and take appropriate action.

The teachers must decide whether to intervene or to ignore. In all too many schools, the teachers choose to ignore.

If a school has changed its culture from "I" to "we" then the teachers have no choice. They feel obligated to intervene. Even though the students are not in their classrooms, and the teachers may not even know who the students are, they do know that they are "our" children. They belong to "our" school and consequently all adults have a responsibility for them. When students know that all of the adults can be counted on to be concerned for them, they experience feelings of safety and security.

Firm, Fair, Consistent, and Positive Discipline

Schools across the world struggle with the creation of appropriate discipline policies, environments and practices. Educators may well spend more time discussing discipline than curriculum or instruction. It is in these discussions about discipline that the frustrations and confusions caused by challenging student behaviour come out. All too often it is in these discussions that the frustration and confusion turns to anger, anger toward colleagues and anger toward the children and their families. A school must come to a consensus about discipline, both philosophically and behaviourally. It must include the belief in and practice of firmness, fairness, consistency and positiveness. For all children to feel safe and secure, a clear schoolwide structure of discipline must be in place.

For years many white educators have worked at being fair and positive. For many noble and not so noble reasons they have emphasised these two aspects of discipline. Unfortunately too many children have been allowed to be less than they could be due to the unwillingness to be firm and consistent. This has been particularly true with children of colour. All children are entitled to a firm and consistent set of behavioural expectations. It is scandalous the degree to which children of colour are not afforded that basic opportunity in our schools.

High Expectations for All Children

Since past two decades we have been aware of the importance of high expectations on the part of adults for student learning. Many have intuitively felt to be true, that children will rise to the level of expectation held for them. Unfortunately, over the years this belief has become mere rhetoric for many educators. It has become an intellectual idea rather than a deeply held belief that is practised.

High expectations that a teacher has for students can be felt by the students. Even visitors to the classroom can feel high expectations. Expectations are communicated in ways that are visceral, that touch our emotions. They touch both our heart and our head. Too many educators don't effectively communicate their high expectations, either because they don't know how or because they don't really have them. For those who don't know how to demonstrate their expectations they can learn. Other educators can help them learn new and effective strategies. But too many educators truly don't believe that all children can learn, and that non-belief is communicated, either overtly or subtly, to the children.

In order for educators to believe that all children can learn, many of them must unlearn some deeply held societal beliefs. They must change the belief that intelligence is fixed at birth. The common thought for many years has been that IQ is innate, fixed and in any population, distributed along a continuum best represented by the bell curve. We must throw out the bell curve as an acceptable operational value for schools.

Learning is developmental process, with the output a combination of the learner's belief in his or her own competence and the investment of hard work. Unfortunately many educators label children early on and respond to them according to the labels they have created. Because intelligence is believed to be innate it follows that when kindergarten children send messages to teachers that indicate 'lower IQ' the response is a lowered expectation. On the other hand if teachers see student potential as developmental, as malleable, as capable of great expansion, then expectations stay high as part of the process of helping students believe in themselves and know that hard work will ensure their "getting smart".

Getting smart, is a process, not an accident of birth. We must abandon the belief that all the ability that a child will ever have comes at birth. We must come to believe in the incredible potential to learn that is present in all children and that potential can be realised in any school and in any classroom, if the right conditions exist. In addition, educators must shed the legacy of racism. All racial, ethnic, and cultural groups have deeply held beliefs about other groups. These beliefs influence educators, particularly in their beliefs about children of colour.

Dedicated Teachers

The work of educating all of our children is too difficult a job to be left to those adults simply seeking employment. Educators must approach the moral challenge of ensuring the educational success of every child with passion, dedication, and enthusiasm. It can no longer be acceptable to "go into teaching" because summers are free, it is an easy second income, or the subject matter is interesting and needs to be shared with young people.

Deciding to go into teaching must be a decision from the heart. It must come from a moral imperative to ensure the success of all children, and from a deeply held commitment to social justice. To be an effective educator today requires far more dedication, talent, and commitment, than ever before. The choice to be an educator must be a proactive choice made by reflective adults, and based upon the moral principal of equity and excellence. Anything less is unacceptable. Our children cannot afford anything but the very best from us.

Multicultural Curriculum

A multicultural curriculum is one that is part of the daily life of a school, part of every subject, and woven into the very fabric of the content of instruction. We must move beyond the textbooks, beyond what we were historically taught and continually seek to be inclusive of diversity in all of our teaching. Every child has the right to feel included. Every child has the right to have the opportunity to feel inclusive of others. This must happen day after day, lesson after lesson. Learning is a process not an event, and learning about diversity is most effective when integrated into the daily life of the classroom.

Outstanding Instructional Practice

Instructional "business as usual" will no longer ensure the success of our children. The profession has come a long way in ascertaining which instructional practices work and which do not. Unfortunately, educational implementation has not caught up with the level of knowledge. Too many educators across the country still teach and administer as if we were living in the 1950's. The schools that work for all children have visionary leaders, working with dedicated and talented teachers applying the instructional practices that research and best practice tell us make significant difference in the education of children.

Developmentally appropriate instruction has to take the place of textbook imposed levels. The human brain is far more complex than our linear curriculum currently recognises. We need to integrate our curricular content utilising interdisciplinary and thematic approaches. We must implement multiple teaching approaches to accommodate the multiple learning styles of students and recognise that there are more that just two kinds of intelligence. School organisations too, need to reflect our increasing awareness that tracking students by ability is a strategy that may make teaching "easier" but does great damage to children.

Outstanding instructional practices have to become commonplace in all of our schools. Our children our society cannot afford to wait any longer. The delaying tactics of many of our educators must stop. Staff development must be fully funded and implemented at all levels. University training programmes must make major systemic changes in the ways that they prepare teachers and principals.

Parental Involvement

Schools that work for all children truly value, appreciate, and seek out parental involvement. They recognise that many parents had negative experiences in school as children themselves. Making parents feel safe valued and wanted takes a proactive set of activities. Creating a more user friendly environment for parents requires educators putting themselves in the parents' perspective.

Parental involvement in a child's education is not a luxury, not just a nice idea. It is not a frill or set of activities engaged in only when time allows. Parental involvement is essential to ensuring all children's success. It is incumbent upon everyone of us to ensure that the home/school partnership becomes part of the very fabric of the school's daily life.

An Effective Mental Health Approach

There is an importance need for recognising the growing psychological and emotional needs of children in our schools. Statistics are chilling as study after study confronts us with a growing amount of poverty, child abuse, substance abuse, and much more. Schools are the places where all of these issues become apparent. Unless these issues are dealt with in an effective manner, children will not be capable of doing the kind of learning that is necessary.

For years we have expected classroom teachers to be part-time counsellors, social workers and parents, as well as full-time teachers. When nuclear families were more intact, when churches were stronger, and when neighbourhoods were more cohesive, the teacher could handle this expectation. Few students needed the teacher to be more than a teacher. Today this is no longer true. Too many students need teachers to play those other roles and teachers simply don't have the time, energy or expertise. The problems have become too large and too pervasive.

In order to assist children with psychological and emotional needs we need skilled professional specialists assisting classroom teachers, parents, and administrators. We need the expertise of mental and physical health professionals. Many schools have formed interdisciplinary and even interagency teams to be that essential resource. These teams are able to address the issues, either individual or systemic, that affect the learning of children. Whether we call them mental health teams that deal with schoolwide issues that may affect mental health, or Student Intervention Teams (SIT) teams that work with individual students using a case management model, the point is that something must be done. The problems have become too great for any one of us to solve and require a concerted team effort.

Pleasing School Environments

Children in alarmingly large numbers live in unclean, unsafe and often frightening environments. School may be the only truly safe place for those children. It is imperative, then, that schools take the necessary steps to ensure that they become the quality safe and attractive places that our children need and deserve them to be. Concerted efforts must be made by school leaders, staffs, parents and community members to provide safe and aesthetically pleasing physical environments. Painted well-maintained and clean school buildings and grounds with a highly visible presence of familiar and caring adults, lets children know that the adults are doing all that they can to make it possible for them to feel safe and free enough to devote all of their attention to learning.

Communities must work to provide a sense of community pride. If schools truly become part of communities (through outreach programmes, adult education programmes, clinics, etc.) then communities will invest ownership and work to keep the schools clean and safe. Schools in some of the poorest neighbourhoods in our country are showpieces of civic pride. These school communities have worked hard to create schools that are centres for the neighbourhood. And it has paid off with block watches, green grass, plants and trees, community painting parties, litter patrols, playground cleanups, and much more.

In this diverse world, creating schools for all children is the right thing to do but it is not easy. It means a major rethinking of the very core values upon which our schools are built. It means an infusion of multiculturalism into the fabric of the schools. It means the inclusion of the excluded. It means rethinking the content and process of curriculum and instruction. It means the integration of disciplines and focusing consciously and specifically on both equity and excellence in the same classrooms in the same schools for all children.

All of us must believe in our very soul that all children can and will learn and that equity and excellence are moral imperatives that can and must be accomplished. We must be prepared to be rebuffed, rebuked, and reviled for standing tall and firm before colleagues, parents, unions, school boards, and society in general. The path to accomplishing a vision of schools for all children will require strong moral and sometimes physical courage. Make no mistake, it will seriously test the mettle of the best of us. It will require an unswerving determination to not be discouraged or detoured and will require enormous amounts of time and energy.

Fundamental Values of Multicultural Curriculum

The fundamental values of any good curriculum are accuracy, completeness, and inclusion. Accuracy and completeness are closely related and refer to the extent to which information presented represents a full picture of a given topic through various sources and perspectives. Inclusion refers to the extent to which different voices and perspectives are in the classroom. There are two levels of inclusion. When most teachers talk about inclusion, they are referring to representational inclusion, or the inclusion of sources or information that closely match or represent the diversity within a particular classroom. A multicultural curriculum encourages them to provide context and perspectives on all subjects covered in school.

While multicultural education recognises the need for some forms of ethnocentric curriculum for students from social identity groups that are currently under— or misrepresented in public school curriculum, multicultural education ultimately aims at dismantling the need for any centric curriculum, as it is inconsistent with the ideals of completeness and accuracy.

The following are the factors led to the curriculum transformation:

i) Ground recommended curricular changes in the larger mission or diversity statements adopted by your college or university.
ii) Be clear about the expected learning goals for diversity courses. Recognise that there are multiple goals for learning about diversity, and take the time to collectively identify priorities important for your students and your community.
iii) Build cross-departmental coalitions early in the process of developing recommended curricular changes. Involve students in curricular change efforts.
iv) Make faculty development that includes both study and dialogue a separate and essential commitment.
v) Explore how curriculum can be strengthened by links to student-life programming.
vi) Recognise both the campus community and the neighboring community as important sites for learning.
vii) Effectively communicate to students and faculty members why students are required to take diversity courses. Put clear language in course catalogs. Explain requirements to students in freshman orientation programmes. Develop orientations for new faculty.
viii) Be aware of potential unintended consequences. The climate in the classroom changes radically when a course becomes "required". Be sure faculty members are prepared for these changes. Incorporate pedagogical issues into faculty development efforts.

Multicultural education as a shift in curriculum, perhaps as simple as adding new and diverse materials and perspectives to be more inclusive of traditionally underrepresented groups. Despite a multitude of differing conceptualisations of multicultural education, several shared ideals provide a basis for its understanding. While some focus on individual students or teachers, and others are much more "macro" in scope, these ideals are all, at their roots, about transformation:

i) Every student must have an equal opportunity to achieve to her or his full potential.

ii) Every student must be prepared to competently participate in an increasingly intercultural society.

iii) Teachers must be prepared to effectively facilitate learning for every individual student, no matter how culturally similar or different from himself.

iv) Schools must be active participants in ending oppression of all types, first by ending oppression within their own walls, then by producing socially and critically active and aware students.

v) Education must become more fully student-centred and inclusive of the voices and experiences of the students.

vi) Educators, activists, and others must take a more active role in reexamining all educational practices and how they affect the learning of all students: testing methods, teaching approaches, evaluation and assessment, school psychology and counseling, educational materials and textbooks, etc.

STRATEGIES FOR TEACHING AND LEARNING

Multicultural education builds on the cultural and ethnic diversity of a society. It values the wealth of multicultural knowledge and skills learners bring to the classroom. It recognises students and their families are not deficient in knowledge, experience and skills, but may have backgrounds that overlap little with what is valued in schools. A curriculum that is multicultural is inclusive. It is informed by the principles that the curriculum is intended for all students and recognises the experience, knowledge and abilities of individual students and their various cultural groups. It acknowledges the diversity of the school community, parents, students and staff, in its services and in its calendar.

An inclusive curriculum encourages students to develop and give voice and legitimacy to their cultural knowledge. Students should examine how something is perceived, communicated, organised, carried out in or would affect their cultures or sub-cultures. They can explore how something is expressed in language, or is brought about in many ways, for example, physically, socially, politically. They develop a dialogue with family and other members of the culture, as well as with fellow students.

Students learn to articulate and explore the sources of their values, attitudes and behaviours. They learn to understand and respect the significance of culture in the construction of these. While certain values are seen as desirable by the community at large, teachers cannot enforce specific values. Teachers set standards of behaviour that encourage respect for everyone. They focus on the development in students of the skills to articulate their values, to recognise the sources of these and to reflect on and make informed choices about values and behaviours. Students negotiate the culture of the classroom and their understandings about the world. They learn to communicate openly and effectively with each other and to accept and value difference. They learn to use cultural diversity as a resource that enriches their work.

Teachers recognise that various intelligences are valued differently in different cultures. Using the curriculum frameworks, teachers should plan teaching and learning activities in culturally appropriate contexts and take into account different intelligences and the learning styles of cultural groups. Following are the learning processes and teaching strategies that achieve multicultural outcomes.

i) Teachers promote the active participation in learning of students with diverse cultural backgrounds and students learning English as a second language.

ii) Teachers plan teaching and learning activities in culturally appropriate contexts.

iii) Teachers provide for all learning styles and the expression of multiple intelligences.

iv) Teachers use language-focused teaching in all lessons because they recognise the critical role of language in learning.

v) Teachers value learning in culturally diverse and in mixed ability groups, so that students learn to share and value the knowledge, skills and talents of others.

vi) Teachers use cooperative learning strategies in a democratic and noncompetitive learning environment and model and demonstrate ways of reaching agreement through negotiation.

vii) Teachers value and support the development of literacy in a first language for itself and for the positive support that developing literacy in a first language offers to the development of literacy in a second.

viii) Teachers share cultural meanings with language learners, for example how intention (expressed in politeness, rudeness, apology, compliment, request, etc.) and nonverbal communication (such as gestures, eye contact or avoidance of it touching the head, passing things with one hand) can be interpreted differently, depending on the cultural context.

ix) Teachers recognise that learning any language and its registers involves interpreting the culture to which it belongs.

The following are the cultural enrichment strategies:

i) Teachers promote a cross-cultural dialogue within the classroom and school.

ii) Teachers invite members of various cultures to share their perspectives and stories, with the understanding that one person does not represent a whole culture.

iii) Teachers avoid stereotypes, making realistic rather than romantic or racist generalisations. They recognise the dangers of perpetuating stereotypes in presenting a slab of culture for study.

iv) Teachers provide for the study of aspects of a culture/s that are closer to those of the students as a bridge to considering aspects of a culture/s that are very different.

v) Teachers focus on intercultural experience and dialogue. They avoid concentrating briefly and only on the surface features of culture.

vi) Teachers promote interaction with members of other cultures through experiences such as pen pals, sister schools, twinned schools and in-country visits.

vii) Teachers and students celebrate each other's cultures, sharing the meanings of festivals and learning to communicate in forms other than words, such as dance, music, art, drama, gesture, facial expression and body language.

Fundamental aspects of culture are represented through the Arts. Arts' criticism and aesthetics, and past and present contexts enable students to appreciate how the arts express important features of their own cultures and those of others. Examples of art forms should be presented in their cultural contexts because people's response to art depends on the roles it plays in their society. In many societies, for example, the primary function of art is religious or spiritual and cannot be understood without reference to religious beliefs and practices. Concentration on surface features of costume, traditional paintings and sculpture or folk dance may reinforce cultural stereotypes.

Texts and their exploration provide a rich source of cultural understanding. Students study texts in which they can recognise themselves and their world, as well as texts from other cultures. Through studying a range of literature, they explore the diversity of culture and how culture is socially constructed. Students also develop an understanding of language by examining how language works in different contexts. Students develop an informed and critical appreciation of their culture in their study of texts and contexts. They explore ways in which their perceptions and responses to text are grounded in the particular sub-cultures of their families and peers, as well as in their broader language and cultural traditions.

Students express their understandings of these influences and explore differences and similarities among them. They enrich their understandings of other cultures through hearing minority voices as they experience and explore texts. Students study the values and messages of texts, and learn to challenge their apparent authority. Teachers explore and build on the existing literacy and learning experiences of students, recognising that in many cases they may not be the same literacy experiences that the school curriculum values.

The multicultural perspective in health and physical education acknowledges that personal development and belonging is grounded in culture. Participation in physical education and sport by all students may be increased by incorporating recreational and physical activities common to the students' cultures into programmes. Parents or older students could be involved in primary schools to teach games from their cultures.

Different cultural values can affect ethical issues. Behaviour in sport, for example, is linked to community beliefs about competition. Students in high schools or colleges can examine the roles of different communities' attitudes in discouraging violence, drink driving, drug-taking and child abuse.

A mathematics curriculum actually reflects the values of the predominant culture. All cultures count, locate, measure and design. They also play games and explain ideas (classifying, validating) in ways critical to mathematical development. The concept of linear time and the emphasis placed on quantity and on accuracy are grounded in Western culture, however. Many cultures do not give these notions such high value. Teachers need to support mathematical concepts by placing them in context and by using concrete materials.

Modern mathematics is the product of many cultures. Teachers can discuss the origins of a specific piece of mathematical knowledge so that students do not assume that all mathematical knowledge is a product of one culture. This will help create positive images of other cultures.

Mathematical ideas embedded in children's stories, oral or written, provide a resource for teachers. These strategies make the curriculum more inclusive and enhance the participation of students from all cultural backgrounds.

Cultures in all parts of the world have traditions of inquiry. They stem from the desire of people to understand their world through observation and form the basis for scientific inquiry. The multicultural perspective gives students an understanding of how science influences different societies and cultures. Students learn about science in their own and other cultures. They can explore how different countries use different science-based technologies for the same task, including responses to global social issues such as overpopulation, pollution and over-consumption of non-renewable resources. Choices are made in response to the demands and values of the society.

Culture should not be treated as a backdrop against which different groups appear but as in what happens every day in the classroom, home, community, nation and beyond. Technological literacy depends on understanding and valuing technologies in their cultural context. Students learn how values, ethics and ideas about technology are formed by cultures, explore how differing ways of life lead to defining problems differently, and examine attitudes to the use of materials and the valuing of different processes, solutions and outcomes.

Students learn that the appropriateness of technology depends on the context within which it will be used. They also examine ethical issues in technological decisions. They come to appreciate the technological achievements of other cultures and times. Technology students compare solutions in different situations. Teachers must ensure that students have equal access to technology and materials.

In some cases, schools may consider providing equipment such as portable computers to be borrowed, with priority being given to those students who would otherwise go without. Toy collections should reflect the multicultural nature of the student population, and schools should provide building materials common in other cultures.

Multiage Grouping

In multiage classrooms, teachers are encouraged to see children as unique individuals, plan for a wide range of abilities, and adjust to individual needs, enabling slower children to catch up to their classmates, without the stigma associated with ability grouping or retention. Multiage grouping foster comparisons and competitiveness among children, research on multiage classrooms has consistently found that such heterogeneous groupings encourage and invite cooperation and pro-social behaviours, such as giving, sharing, taking turns, and sensitivity.

Children's friendships, both in classrooms and in naturalistic settings, have been one theme of the multiage research. In fact, research overwhelmingly favours multiage grouping because of its positive effects on children's social and emotional development and on the classroom climate. Researchers have reported improved self-esteem, self-concept as a learner, reduced anxiety, and improved attitudes toward school

Multiage classrooms frequently experience fewer discipline problems. Multiage grouping in a multilingual classroom also holds the potential for providing additional linguistic role models for children. In addition, the act of teaching a younger child helps an older child deepen his or her own understanding of a subject, at the same time that the younger child is helped to engage in more complex activities. Of course, teachers need to ensure that older children do not overwhelm younger children and that younger children do not become a burden to their older classmates. In addition, ensuring that older children are sufficiently challenged by the curriculum is an important consideration.

Clearly, multiage classrooms offer many advantages, including fewer retentions, positive effects on children's social and emotional development, an improved social climate, and more individualised attention. Teachers often report an enhanced sense of professionalism and efficacy. When children are encouraged to learn at their own pace in a supportive, family-like environment, they are free to develop their interests and learning styles, without fear of failure.

Educators who have implemented multiage classrooms have identified a number of factors that influence the success of such programmes. Educators are unanimous in advising that top-down mandates are ineffective in creating a positive and supportive climate of change. Also central to the success of multiage grouping is a curriculum that is flexible and responsive to children's individual needs and strengths. While children may sometimes be grouped homogeneously to learn basic skills within the context of authentic activities, the majority of the day should be spent in activities that maximise the benefits of interaction and cooperation among children.

Advocates of multiage grouping emphasise the family-like atmosphere, in which younger family members have many opportunities to observe and imitate the competencies of older members, and as a method of maintaining family bonding. In addition, a number of researchers have pointed out that children live increasingly in an age-segregated society—in child care and schools—and spend less time with families and in neighbourhoods, which include a range of ages.

Development of Multicultural Competencies

The provision of relevant multicultural curriculums, the use of culturally sensitive assessment and intervention strategies, the training of school staff in the provision of these services, the recruitment and retention of multicultural and diverse professionals, and the integration of diverse communities and parents in an authentic and empowering manner are only a few of the critical issues facing those working with today's students. Professionals are also challenged by the need to consider the impact of complex social/environmental problems, which in many contexts have negative consequences for children from various racial/ethnic and social class backgrounds.

Although there has clearly been a greater recognition of the need for training in multicultural competence across professions, many programmes still conceptualise this training as more of an "add-on"; that is, programmes require only one or two courses for their particular professional speciality. This is in contrast to a more comprehensive and integrated "paradigm shift" in the teaching of all helping professional courses.

The training of school staff and other related professionals can be conceptualised by using a model that emphasises three major components: awareness, knowledge, and skills. The awareness component involves professionals examining their own values, myths, stereotypes, and world view. Knowledge entails developing a non-stereotyping, flexible understanding of cultural, social, and family dynamics of diverse groups, along with a comprehension of the critical sociopolitical, historical, and economic contexts in which people from diverse multicultural groups are embedded. Skills require the development of culturally sensitive, flexible, and empowering treatment and assessment strategies that are accompanied by communication skills, the integration of multicultural and diversity issues in various treatment modalities, multicultural consultation, and advocacy skills.

A useful model that allows for the integration of many of these critical variables is the Ecological Model developed by Bronfenbrenner. According to this model, try to understand or evaluate a student (the microsystem) in the context of his mesosystems (immediate family, extended family, friends, network), macrosystems (culture or subculture), and exosystems (social structures). This model places the diverse learner, school staff, and parents/community in an ecological context, which then allows both for a broader understanding of the critical issues affecting students from diverse backgrounds and the development of relevant service and educational models.

These educational models need to be highly sensitive to the particular community and social contexts of which the diverse learners and school staff are members. For the diverse learner and the school staff, the ability to conceptualise and integrate culture and issues of diversity within a developmental perspective is also crucial, given the changes in developmental tasks at each life stage and the various ways that these "tasks" are expressed and resolved within various cultural groups.

Through the development of multicultural competencies within the areas of awareness, knowledge, and skills, the probability increases of psychologists using assessment and treatment strategies that meet the needs of a wide range of culturally diverse groups. The need for flexible and culturally sensitive assessment techniques has continued to be stressed by many in the field. Examinations of the critical features in assessment should include the sociocultural context of the diverse learner and his family, the sociocultural background of the examiner, such as issues of awareness of biases and stereotypes, and the selection of appropriate testing, interview, and survey instruments.

The need for changes in the conceptualisation of children's abilities and how skills are assessed, particularly with diverse learners, has also led to strategies that focus on problem-solving abilities. With the changing composition of today's student population, the need to provide educational programmes that address the complex issues related to multiculturalism and diversity is becoming more and more evident. Schools and educators must begin to develop curriculums that integrate awareness, knowledge, and skills within educational materials. It is critical that diversity and multiculturalism not be conceived as being accomplished by adding a course, a lecture, or a one-day "multicultural fair'.

A total curriculum transformation needs to take place where the critical issues of diversity and multiculturalism are integrated into all aspects of students' academic achievement, social skills development, and relationship with the community at large. The opportunity for children to begin to integrate into their lives issues related to multiculturalism and diversity is vital to the development of acceptance and respect for others from diverse backgrounds. Under this general category of enhancing multicultural awareness and respect for diversity is the critical need for confronting issues of racism and prejudice.

Another major component in working with diverse learners is that of establishing "authentic" relationships with parents and the community. This is a critical element of any effort directed towards increasing multicultural understanding and the development of a truly pluralistic school and community environment.

References

Cortes, C. E., "Future will demand culturally literate citizens", *Thrust for Educational Leadership*, 7(3), 20-22, 1978,

Gollnick, D. M., Chinn, P. C., *Multicultural Education in a Pluralistic Society,* St. Louis: Mosby, 1990.

Gay, G., "Curriculum for multicultural education", In F. H. Klassen and D. M. Gollnick (eds.), *Pluralism and the American teacher: Issues and Case Studies,* Washington, DC: American Association of Colleges for Teacher Education, 1977.

Ramirez, M. and Castaneda, A., *Cultural Democracy, Bicognitive Development and Education*, New York: Academic Press, 1974.

Pederson, P. and J. C. Carey (eds.), *Multicultural Counseling in Schools: A Practical Handbook,* Boston, MA: Allyn & Bacon, 1994.

Omizo, M. M., and D'Andrea, M. J., "Multicultural classroom guidance", In C. C. Lee (ed.), *Counseling for diversity: A guide for school counselors and related professionals,* Boston, MA: Allyn & Bacon, 1995.

3

Culturally Relevant and Caring Teacher

From the early part of the twentieth century, theories of cultural discontinuity have been proposed in an attempt to explain the difficulty encountered by students in adapting to a school environment foreign to the societal norms of their ethnic community. But creating a culturally responsive and relevant learning environment can only be achieved through indepth work.

A number of strategies can help all concerned gain the self-awareness needed to begin a classroom conversation on the deeply-held, often taken-for-granted beliefs and biases that make up the ecology of the classroom and society. Using multicultural literature dealing with issues pertaining to race, class, gender, or disability can teach children to think critically and, at the same time, build a democratic classroom and school.

Instead, the suggested approach is to view multicultural education as a perspective that is integrated into the daily activities of the classroom. If it begins with teachers' self-reflection, it also includes an examination of biased attitudes and behaviours that are structured into our society and our schools, and an exploration and validation of the many cultures that make up the classroom, our nation and our world.

Creating a culturally safe environment approach is the assumption that diverse languages and ways of understanding and interpreting the world are an asset and a resource, not a liability. In order for children to construct a "knowledgeable, confident, self-identity", schools must stop requiring children to "subtract" their language and cultural identity and replace it with the language and culture of the dominant group, a process known as assimilation. Rather, they must acknowledge and build on cultural differences, while at the same time preparing children to live successfully in both worlds—their home culture and the larger society.

A wide variety of multicultural learning activities ensures that all children see themselves and their families reflected in the classroom environment. The role of public education has been not only to produce future workers but to socialise students into the existing social, economic, and political ideologies by transmitting knowledge, skills, and social and moral rules of the culture.

Even when teachers cannot speak the language of all children in the classroom, they can communicate to children and parents that their language and culture are valued within the context of the school. For example, learning as many words as possible in a linguistically diverse child's language, encouraging children to teach the class a few words in their language, and providing bilingual signs around the classroom convey to children and their families that diverse languages are valued. Colour-coding the signs with a different colour for each language draws children's attention to the different languages used in labelling.

Learning a new language is a huge task, for both children and adults. While many educators believe that young children learn a new language with little effort, studies of the process reveal that mastering a new language takes time, perseverance, and support from adults and peers.

Developing strong family/school partnerships is essential to providing cultural continuity for children. Encouraging children to bring pictures of their families and share favourite stories or songs from home, and asking family members to share aspects of their culture, can help children feel secure and valued for who they are. Parents and other family and community members may be encouraged to visit the school to read, tell stories, and share oral traditions, beliefs and values, and knowledge of traditional celebrations, art, music, poetry, and dance.

It is important to respect a family's beliefs about sharing their culture and language; some families may feel that this practice is intrusive. It is also important to help children be comfortable with their parents' visits. Since English is a high-status language, children may learn early that other languages are less valued, and feel ashamed of their home language and culture.

By understanding the way children learn a first language, teachers can apply these principles to help children learn English. While until recently English-as-a-Second-Language (ESL) methods of teaching had a strong behaviouristic skills orientation, current practices emphasise a whole language approach. ESL literature identifies attainment of communicative competence as the goal of instruction. With the recognition that language is best learned through actual use in a nonthreatening social context, language use is encouraged by focusing on meaning rather than correctness of form, regarding errors as part of the learning process.

Like young children learning a first language, when children's communicative attempts are directly corrected, they may learn that it is better not to speak at all. Modelling the correct form and encouraging further communication help children gain proficiency without damaging their self-esteem. Teachers can help children connect new words with meaning by using contextual cues, such as gestures, actions, pictures, and real objects.

Using lots of poems, chants, and songs that include repetition of phrases helps children learn vocabulary and knowledge of story structure within enjoyable activities. Poetry and songs are fun to memorise and can last a lifetime. Unusual vocabulary and complex word structures are often taken in stride when they appear in songs and poetry.

Cultural incongruities between the patterns of communication experienced by children in the home and at school can undermine successful learning. For example, many classrooms emphasise individual responsibility and achievement, competition, and teacher controlled learning.

TEACHING WITH A MULTICULTURAL PERSPECTIVE

Teaching with a multicultural perspective encourages appreciation and understanding of other cultures as well as one's own. Teaching with this perspective promotes the child's sense of the uniqueness of his own culture as a positive characteristic and enables the child to accept the uniqueness of the cultures of others. Children's attitudes toward their race and ethnic group and other cultural groups begin to form early in the preschool years. Infants can recognise differences in those around them, and young children can easily absorb negative stereotypes.

Children are easily influenced by the culture, opinions, and attitudes of their caregivers. Caregivers' perceptions of ethnic and racial groups can affect the child's attitudes toward those minority groups. Early childhood educators can influence the development of positive attitudes in young children by learning about and promoting the various cultures represented among the children they teach. Young children can develop stereotypic viewpoints of cultures different from their own when similarities among all individuals are not emphasised.

Teachers can help eliminate stereotypes by presenting material and activities that enable children to learn the similarities of all individuals. Circle time is particularly helpful in this respect, as it provides children with a feeling of group identity and introduces them to the variety of cultures represented in the class. A multicultural programme should not focus on other cultures to the exclusion of the cultures represented in the class. Children from different cultures often have to make major behavioural adjustments to meet the expectations of the school.

Teachers should take whatever measures are necessary to see that children do not interpret these adjustments as evidence of cultural stereotypes. Early childhood teachers and parents of young children should become aware of the myths associated with multicultural education so that they can enhance developmentally appropriate practices. The emphasis on so-called exotic differences will often accentuate a "we" versus "they" polarity. Children who are not able to identify with another culture because of exotic differences will often feel superior or inferior to the culture.

A multicultural programme can focus on the presentation of other cultures, but at the same time allow children to be aware of the nature and uniqueness of their own culture. Children can learn about their class as an example of a common culture. Recent studies suggest that, all other things being equal, higher degrees of bilingualism are associated with higher levels of cognitive attainment. It is evident that the duality of languages per se does not hamper the overall language proficiency or cognitive development of bilingual children.

Our world is multicultural, and children need to experience the diversity outside their immediate environment. If children are to know about minority groups, they must be taught about them in the same way they are taught about majority groups. Otherwise, children can grow to adulthood unaware of, and insensitive to, the experiences of other cultural groups.

Since we have a multitude of cultures in our world, it is impractical, perhaps impossible, to teach about all of them. Goals and curriculum will, therefore, differ considerably from class to class. It is important for early childhood teachers and parents to acknowledge that everyone has a culture, not just those who appear to be different. Children who are taught to appreciate and understand their own culture learn to understand others' cultures in the process.

Multicultural education embodies a perspective rather than a curriculum. Teachers must consider children's cultural identities and be aware of their own biases. One problem with the current thrust in multicultural education is that it pays little or no attention to teaching people how to recognise when culturally and racially different groups are being victimised by the racist or biased attitudes of the larger society. In order to change people's oppressive ways, we must learn about oppression.

Teachers and parents can take several approaches to integrate and develop a multicultural perspective. The promotion of a positive self-concept is essential, as is a focus on activities that highlight the similarities and differences of all children's lives. Children's play, particularly role play, is an excellent strategy for developing new perspectives on culture and lifestyles. The treatment of children as unique individuals, each with something special to contribute, is an important strategy. If a teacher is to understand the whole child, he or she must become aware of the child's cultural background.

Children can benefit from understanding the teacher's heritage and background. The feeling of connection that results is vital to the child's acceptance of the similarities and differences of others. Through multicultural literature, children discover that all cultural groups have made significant contributions to civilisation. A well-balanced multicultural literature programme includes literature that depicts people with a variety of aspirations, from different sociometric levels, with different occupations, and with a range of human characteristics.

Functions of a Multicultural Teacher

Areas within the educational setting in which multicultural education is implemented are textbooks and instructional materials, curriculum and instruction, teacher behaviour, and school climate. How teachers use textbooks and other instructional materials is extremely important in providing multicultural education. Teachers need to recognise subtle as well as blatant forms of bias such as invisibility, stereotyping, selectivity and imbalance, unreality, fragmentation and isolation, and language.

Invisibility means that certain microcultures, including disability groups, are underrepresented in materials. This omission implies that these groups have less value, importance, and significance in our society.

Stereotyping assigns traditional and rigid roles or attributes to a group. Stereotyping occurs across cultural and exceptionality groups.

Selectivity and imbalance occur when issues and situations are interpreted from only one perspective, usually the perspective of the majority group.

Unreality is most likely to present itself in the portrayal of history and contemporary life experiences. Controversial topics are glossed over, and discussions of discrimination and prejudice are avoided. This unrealistic coverage denies children the information needed to recognise, understand, and perhaps conquer the problems that plague our society. Contemporary problems faced by individuals with disabilities and those from diverse racial and ethnic groups are often disguised or simply not included.

Fragmentation and isolation occur when publishers discuss issues, contributions, and information about various groups in a separate section or chapter apart from the regular text. This add-on approach suggests that the experiences and contributions of these groups are merely an interesting diversion, not an integral part of historical and contemporary developments.

Language bias occurs when materials blatantly omit such things as gender, disability, or ethnic group references.

A teacher's behaviour in the classroom is a key factor in helping all students reach their potential, regardless of gender, ethnicity, age, religion, language, or exceptionality. Unknowingly, educators often transmit biased messages to students. Most educators do not consciously or intentionally stereotype students or discriminate against them; they usually try to treat all students fairly and equitably. When teachers are able to recognise the subtle and unintentional biases in their behaviour, positive changes can be made in the classroom.

Another area that teachers might investigate and change to better meet the needs of a culturally diverse student population is that of teaching and learning styles. Both teaching and learning styles can be categorised as either field independent or field sensitive. Field-independent teachers encourage independent student achievement and competition among students. Field-sensitive teachers are more interpersonally oriented and prefer situations that allow them to use personal, conversational techniques. Similarly, field-sensitive students perform better in social situations such as group work; field-independent students work well on independent projects. Often the teacher's style differs from the learning style of the student, causing a classroom situation that may not be conducive to helping students reach their potential.

A school that affirms multiculturalism will integrate the community in its total programme. Not only will the educators know and understand the community, but the parents and community will know and participate in the school activities. The first step in multiculturalising the school is development of positive and supportive relations between the school and the community. Teachers can assist by asking community members to participate in class activities by talking about their jobs, hobbies, or experiences in a certain area. They can initiate contacts with families of students. They can participate in some community events. A sincere interest in the community, rather than indifference or patronage, will help to bridge the gap that often exists between the school and community.

Teachers in multicultural classrooms must be open to their students and put forth the effort needed to get to know their students inside and outside of class. If a teacher is hesitant about being open, the class will reciprocate and the students will become estranged from one another and the teacher. In order to be open, teachers must be interested in their students, fearless, willing to try new and different things, sure of themselves in order to avoid taking things personally, and non-judgmental of his or her students. Also, openness is not making assumptions and being prepared for the unexpected. Many cultures have many different mores and folkways. Teachers must be open to what the students are doing and find out why they do what they do. This openness will create communication in the class, which will ultimately develop into a classroom that is learning, understanding, and culturally fluent.

In addition to openness, teachers must know the learning patterns of the students in their class. They must understand the learning patterns of the students who grew up in a culture other than their own.

The best way to handle culture clash is to be open, knowledgeable, and not be afraid to talk about the cultural differences in class no matter what discipline the teacher is teaching. An open teacher will create an open class and an open class will have open lines of communication that will create a positive and beneficial learning environment for everyone.

Language difference is another major issue that teachers must address when establishing a multicultural classroom. A teacher who tries to learn the native tongue of her or his students, if only a word or two, will convey respect for the culture of his or her students and increase their potentially suffering self-esteem. Introducing the language or culture of all students in the class into the curriculum will communicate that students of that culture are important.

In order to establish a respect for other cultures in the classroom, teachers must move beyond "multicultural moments" or pseudo-multiculturalism.

One very simple way for all teachers to add multicultural ideas and content to his or her curriculum is to build a classroom library of multicultural literature. No matter what subject you teach you can build a library of books by and/or about different cultures.

Incorporating multicultural literature in to the class is very important, if teachers do not do this they will fall into a trap of buying "the book that has always been used" or "a book that is good enough." Thoughts like those will lead teachers to a sad day when they're packing up all their books on the last day of school and suddenly they realise that they have been sending a message to their students that only White people exist in Math. This is the message that many students are getting today, no matter if they are White, Black, Asian and Hispanic, etc., that teachers must do away with.

Teachers who own literature by authors form different backgrounds is great but it is not enough. True multicultural activities must be ongoing and integrated daily in both informal and formal activities.

Gloria Boutte and Christine McCormick suggest six basic principles for teachers to use when evaluating their culturally diverse classroom, these are:

i) building multicultural programmes,

ii) showing appreciation of differences,

iii) avoiding stereotypes,

iv) acknowledging differences in children,

v) discovering the diversity within the classroom,

vi) avoiding pseudo-multiculturalism.

Showing appreciation of differences is very important because a teacher who does not show appreciation of all the differences in their class will not get the chance to attempt any of the other five principles. Teachers need to pay attention to their verbal and non-verbal language when he or she responds to students who speak differently. For example, if a child reads, "Dere go the sto-man," the teacher should avoid interrupting the student to provide the correct English version. Instead, the teacher should thank the student for reading and then model the correct English version when she or he speaks. However, the most important thing to remember about all classrooms is the premise that every child is unique. All children are different and beautiful in their own way, no one student should feel excluded from the class especially if the reason they feel they are excluded is based on race, ethnicity, or colour. Teachers need to show the colour of our world every time they enter a classroom whether maths, science, art, or physical education.

An important step in teaching children to be comfortable with their cultural background and essentially themselves is to encourage and value their input in a small group of other students. This has to do with the organisation of the classroom and the development of lesson plans. When grouping students, teachers should put students from differing backgrounds together. The term "differing backgrounds" refers to (in general) two types of students from two different learning styles. Students who are from a socialised culture that prioritises group achievement, cooperation, obedience, and respect toward authority tend to be externally motivated, dependent on praise and reinforcement from significant others, and more responsive to a socially oriented curriculum.

Countries that teach using a social structure and curriculum include Israel, Germany, and Italy. While students who are from cultures that emphasise individualism, assertiveness, personal initiative, and material well-being tend to be analytical, competitive, impersonal, and task-oriented. Although it is imperative that students be considered on an individual basis, students will tend to be more like one category than the other. Grouping socially-oriented children with children who are task-oriented and impersonal allows the teacher to confront, explore, and celebrate difference.

An accomplished teacher should be able to create projects for a group of students from different backgrounds that will require students to work together, therefore allowing each student to be an important part of the group and learn information through the interaction of the group. Lesson plans that can do this and interest students will become invaluable for teachers to posses as the need for teachers to become culturally fluent continues to grow. Creating multicultural classrooms is a growing priority for all teachers and administrators. This includes restructuring classroom evaluation and punishment techniques, but, more importantly, it includes embracing difference and opening up the classroom for communication.

Importance of Critical Teacher Reflection

Critical teacher reflection is essential to culturally relevant pedagogy because it can ultimately measure teachers' levels of concern and care for their students. A teacher's willingness to ask tough questions about his own attitudes toward diverse students can reflect a true commitment that the individual has toward students' academic success and emotional well-being. A number of scholars have included the concept of care as a critical component of effective teaching.

One of the most fundamental features of culturally responsive teaching is the power of caring. Caring is frequently manifested through teacher attitudes, expectations and behaviours. There area number of considerations teachers must keep in mind in a critical reflection process. Teachers should examine class data on an ongoing basis and ask deep-seated questions about equity in the classroom.

Thus, teachers should be mindful of how their actions can contribute to the development of a consciousness that is emancipatory and has social and cultural relevance. Conversely, teachers who refuse to monitor their own beliefs and classroom ethos can contribute to resistance on the part of students. Recognising that all facets of teaching carry explicit and implicit political implications should result in ongoing reflection to clarify the educational agenda that is being promoted within a classroom setting.

The racial and cultural incongruence between students and teachers may be another factor that explains school failure of students of colour. Teacher practice and thought must be reconceptualised in a manner that recognises and respects the intricacies of cultural and racial difference. Teachers must construct pedagogical practices in ways that are culturally relevant, racially affirming, and socially meaningful for their students.

The term critical reflection attempts to look at reflection within moral, political, and ethical contexts of teaching. Issues pertaining to equity, access, and social justice are typically ascribed to critical reflection . Critical reflection is the type of processing that is crucial to the concept of culturally relevant pedagogy.

Reflective action can be a more useful tool for addressing social and emotional issues, namely, those issues pertaining to race and culture. One of the central tenets of culturally relevant teaching is a rejection of deficit-based thinking about culturally diverse students. One of the central principles of culturally relevant pedagogy is an authentic belief that students from culturally diverse and low-income backgrounds are capable learners.

To become culturally relevant, teachers need to engage in honest, critical reflection that challenges them to see how their positionality influences their students in either positive or negative ways. Critical reflection should include an examination of how race, culture, and social class shape students' thinking, learning, and various understandings of the world.

There are three areas that should be essential components toward the development of culturally relevant teaching practices.

i) teachers must acknowledge how deficit-based notions of diverse students continue to permeate traditional school thinking, practices, and placement, and critique their own thoughts and practices to ensure they do not reinforce prejudice behaviour.
ii) culturally relevant pedagogy recognises the explicit connection between culture and learning, and sees students' cultural capital as an asset and not a detriment to their school success.
iii) culturally relevant teaching is mindful of how traditional teaching practices reflect middle-class,

cultural values, and thus seeks to incorporate a wider range of dynamic and fluid teaching practices.

Effective reflection of race within a diverse cultural context requires teachers to engage in one of the more difficult processes for all individuals—honest self-reflection and critique of their own thoughts and behaviours. Critical reflection requires one to seek deeper levels of self-knowledge, and to acknowledge how one's own worldview can shape students' conceptions of self. Critical reflection can be useful in helping teachers recognise if they consciously or subconsciously subscribe to deficit-based notions of culturally diverse students.

The formation of a culturally relevant teaching paradigm becomes extremely difficult, if not impossible, without critical reflection. The nature of critical reflection can be an arduous task because it forces the individual to ask challenging questions that pertain to one's construction of individuals from diverse racial, ethnic, and cultural backgrounds.

As the teaching profession becomes increasingly homogeneous, given the task of educating an increasingly heterogeneous student population, reflections on racial and cultural differences are essential. In order to become a culturally relevant pedagogue, teachers must be prepared to engage in a rigorous and oftentimes painful reflection process about what it means to teach students who come from different racial and cultural backgrounds than their own.

An antiracist pedagogy requires teachers to adopt a commitment to thinking, feeling, and acting in ways that combats racial discrimination in schools. There are four key steps in developing an anti-racist pedagogy:

i) develop deeper self-knowledge about one's racial and cultural identity, and how racism has shaped this identity;

ii) acquire a new information base about the role that race and racism play in various educational policies and practices;

iii) de-centre and extend empathy to increase one's knowledge base about racially and culturally diverse groups; and

iv) become activists to develop skills and competence to combat racial inequities in work, school, and community settings.

Teachers must be careful to not allow racial classifications of students to be used as rigid and reductive cultural characteristics. A critical reflection process enables teachers to recognise the vast array of differences that can exist within groups. Teachers must avoid creating stereotypical profiles of students that may only do more harm than good. While there may be central tendencies shown within groups, teachers should develop individual profiles of students based on students' own thoughts and behaviours.

References

Bennett, C., *Comprehensive multicultural education: Theory and practice,* Massachusetts: Allen & Bacon, 1995.

Banks, J. A., *Diversity within Unity: Essential Principles for Teaching and Learning in a Multicultural Society*, CME Publications, University of Washington, Seattle, 1995.

Dimidjian, V.J., "Holiday, Holy Days, and Wholly Dazed", *Young Children*, 1989.

Dixon, G.T., Fraser, S., "Teaching Preschoolers in a Multilingual Classroom", *Childhood Education*, 1986.

Hakuta, K., Garcia, E., "Bilingualism and Education", *American Psychologist*, 1989.

Kagan, S.L., Garcia, E.E., "Educating Culturally and Linguistically Diverse Preschoolers: Moving the Agenda", *Early Childhood Research Quarterly*, 1991.

Klassen, F. H., and D. M. Gollnick (eds.), *Pluralism and the American teacher: Issues and Case Studies,* Washington, DC: American Association of Colleges for Teacher Education, 1977.

Lee, C. C. (ed.), *Counseling for diversity: A guide for school counselors and related professionals,* Boston, MA: Allyn & Bacon, 1995.

Norton, D.E., "Language and Cognitive Development Through Multicultural Literature", *Childhood Education*, 1985.

Phillips, C.B., "Nurturing Diversity For Today's Children and Tomorrow's Leaders", *Young Children*, 1988.

4

Dynamics of Cultural Transmission

International migrations develop and a growing number of foreign groups settle in the great cities of the developed or developing countries. Due to the new facilities of telecommunication, it is easy for migrants to maintain contacts with their home countries: it gives to their cultures more chance to survive. In the past, multicultural situations were tolerated by the ruling groups, but their aim was generally to integrate minority groups into mainstream cultures. In order to understand the problems of today, it is worth to investigate the dynamics of modern civilisations and the reason for which multiculturalism arose as an answer to the emerging spatial pattern of cultures.

Cultures are not static realities. They are dynamic ones. During the first half of the twentieth century, anthropologists often conceived cultures as superorganic realities which were enforced on everybody in a society. Today cultures are generally considered as resulting from a complex process of handing on the practices and knowledge of older generations and taking advantage of personal experience: since everyone is exposed to a different set of models and has a different life trajectory, what he learns is not exactly equivalent to what has been internalised by other persons.

In this perspective, cultures appear as complex sets of practices, attitudes, knowhows, knowledge, beliefs and values. They are plastic realities: everyone reinterprets constantly what it has received or experienced in order to deal with evolving environments. Culture establishes strong links between the individual and the collective past since much of it has been inherited. It is geared to the present thanks to personal experience.

Identities play a decisive role in the dynamics of culture, since they limit some forms of evolution, and favour others. Values and identities give some measure of permanency to cultures, when horizons of expectation undermines their stability, since they introduce diverging tendencies on the social scene. Cultures are built thanks to the passing over of attitudes, practices, know hows, knowledge, beliefs and values from an individual to the other, from one generation to the next. They depend upon the channels and means of communication used by the groups under scrutiny.

The transmission and permanent reappraisal of cultures may result from direct visual observation and verbal interaction. They may be at least partially passed over through the written word. In the contemporary world, telecommu-nications play a growing role. Direct face-to-face communication is perfectly efficient for the handing over of gestures, practices or know hows. Modern telecommunications combine the long range of the written word and the advantages of orality and direct imitation low and high cultures. The content of cultures differs according to the prevailing means of communication upon which they rely. An opposition existed in the past between low and high cultures.

Low cultures differed often widely from an area to the next since they relied on low range mechanisms of communication. The high cultures depended mainly on the written. In order to build more secure memories, some oral cultures maintained specialists in this field, bards for instance. The blossoming of high cultures occured however generally after the introduction of writing. Their content was different from that of low cultures : they were poor on the material dimensions of daily life, either productive or domestic. In the field of social life, they stressed rules more than customs and habits. Religious beliefs were generally central to them. They allowed for the development of intellectual activities, letters, arts and sciences.

High cultures presented often similar features over wide areas, since they were built on writing, which is a long range communication mean. They were evidently many relations between the low and high cultures existing within an area. High cultures classes tried to transform local low cultures by imposing their own form of belief and religious system. The opposition between low and high cultures was parallel to the existence of class structures, even if the two forms of division did not coincide exactly.

A new dichotomy has been substituted, during the twentieth century, for the old opposition between low and high cultures: the opposition between mass cultures and specialised and technical ones. Due to the growing role of radio, movies and television, the passing over of gestures, attitudes or know-hows through visual imitation and oral communication has ceased to be limited to small areas. The low cultures of the past are replaced by mass cultures. Their content is different and they are more centred on consumption than production, entertainment than work.

High cultures are transformed. They incorporate a larger share of scientific knowledge and techniques than before and give less room to rhetorics, philosophy or religion. The new specialised and technical cultures do not play the same role as the traditional high cultures in the field of ethics and social regulation. They appear as subservient to the society as a whole, and are not intended to rule over it. The new couple mass cultures/specialised or technical techniques is the translation in the field of culture of the process of globalisation.

Culture is a useful tool to describe the luggage of know-hows, attitudes, knowledge and beliefs societies use in order to hold a grip over their environment and organise human interaction. When consideration is given to its normative and religious components, and to its role in the building of identities, it gives also insights into the way sets of uncoordinated attitudes and techniques are transformed into systems, with their own dynamics.

To deal with the cultural dimension of social life, another concept has to be used—civilisation. During the first millenium B.C., the agricultural societies of the Middle East, India and China were already deeply socially differenciated. A part of their population lived in cities. They had strong armies. States existed, with sophisticated political forms of organisation. The authority of monarchs or emperors generally rested on a religious basis. During this period, new forms of religious or philosophical beliefs appeared independently in Palestine, Iran, Greece, India or China, specially around 500 B.C.: Judaism in Palestine, Zoroastrianism in Iran, Buddhism in India, Confucianism and Taoism in China, the metaphysics of Reason in Greece. These movements differed by many of their features, but shared a new perspective.

The foundations of religious life changed—instead of being imanent, they became transcendent. It gave to the high cultures of the axial societies a new dimension—because of their transcendental dimensions, their religious or philosophical beliefs did not explain the world as it was. It showed how it had to be transformed. The dynamics of high cultures became a dynamics of self achievement and surpassing. Religious life ceased to be aimed at the smooth functioning of man/milieu relationships and social life. People were asked to transform themselves in order to get a higher status in an other world. It meant also that they had to change the world. Due to their transcendental basis, many of the axial societies developed a universalist dimension.

In its relation with other cultures and societies, western civilisation benefited from many advantages. The idea of progress had been translated into a search for material performances in the field of economic activities. It was conducive to the development of new technologies and the improvement of the material conditions of life. Everyone all over the world grew conscious of this situation—new products and new types of consumption were rapidly incorporated into the low culture components of non-western societies. The horizons of expectation of most of their population incorporated an increasing share of images and dreams coming from developed countries.

Since the western civilisation was by now mainly based on the idea of progress, it appeared as a lay civilisation—its values could apparently be adopted without renouncing to the locally prevailing religious faith. Hence the temptation, for many members of the elites of non-western societies, to incorporate in their beliefs a part of the western ideas. In order to achieve progress, a deep transformation of the former value systems had indeed to be achieved.

When people moved from a traditional society to the modernised western countries, either the United States, Canada, the other British Dominions, Argentina, Brazil or France, which attracted the main migration streams from the mid 19th century, they generally shared one of the low cultures of their home countries, but were not acquainted with their high components, except in the religious field. In their host countries, they were offered the possibility to integrate a more open form of high culture without renouncing to their personal religious beliefs. Their children benefited from good school systems. Integration into the host society and culture was the aim of the majority of migrants.

Mass migration was conducive to a higher occurrence of multicultural situations in developed countries, but most of them appeared as transitory. Globalisation, the crisis of western civilisation and the proliferation of multicultural situations and multicultural ideologies. Due to globalisation, the diffusion of innovations, consumptions patterns and new daily life patterns which was active from mid-nineteenth century gained a new momentum during the last 50 years. Mortality experienced a sharp decline everywhere after the end of World War II, inducing progressively new attitudes towards procreation and life : the reduction of fertility rates appareared as a necessity, which generally meant a sharp break with previous religious attitudes.

In many respects, a process of standardisation is at work in the cultural field. It results from the impact of mass cultures and the diffusion of new consumption patterns at the world scale. Production technologies have ceased to be included in the sphere of low cultures or their contemporary counterparts, mass cultures. They are increasingly incorporated into the new forms of high cultures, i.e., the technological or scientific ones. Since they rest on scientific knowledge and technologies, they are conducive to the uniformisation of tools, machine tools and products. The material content of culture is more uniform than in the past.

The standardisation of cultures is one of most striking features of today world. This process undermines however the bases of most identities. Cultures differed traditionally from place to place, technologies varied from a town to the next one and crafts were so long to acquire that people stick to the same job for all their life. People had the feeling to belong to the same group because they lived in the same type of house, ate the same food, drank the same beverages, wore the same dress, and looked at landscapes which mirrored the agricultural technologies they used and their past history. Standardisation has rubbed out a good part of the traditional identity markers.

At a time of mass cultures, young people are wearing the same jeans and dancing according to the same rhythms all over the world. As a result, globalisation triggered strong reactions. People refuse to look like their neighbours. They protect the landscapes of the countries they live in, preserve their monuments and try to avoid a complete standardisation of the food and beverage locally produced.

Identities were not based only on material markers. They were also—and generally mainly—anchored in the values shared by individuals and communities. In the pursuit of development, some of the values imported with the western ideology of progress proved contradictory with the central beliefs of the local non-western religions. The new facilities of transport and communication allowed for a rapid transformation of the horizons of expectation of ordinary people all over the world.

The threat over identities resulting from globalisation has fueled many types of ideological or religious movements during the last thirty years—ecologisms, regionalisms, nationalisms or fundamentalisms. In western countries there always were people sceptical with the idea of progress. They knew that the improvement of the material conditions of life would not necessarily be conducive to the control of passions and a better moral life.

Due to the increasing mobility of persons and the easier transfer of information, the contacts between cultures are closer than in the past. Migration from the south countries to the rich ones of the North appear to many individuals as the only way to escape local poverty and instability and to materialise their horizons of expectation. People do not move because western civilisation appears a superior one to them. Their personal situations differ from those prevailing in the past. Due to the generalisation of primary and secondary education, a growing proportion of migrants is familiar with the traditional high cultures of their home country. Due to the modernisation of local consumption patterns and modes of life, the gap between the material cultures of the home and host countries has been reduced.

Emigrants have ceased to be motivated by the search of a higher and better civilisation. They move because they wish to get a job, earn higher salaries and enjoy better social security systems. Due to more rapid and cheaper transport, and new telecommunication technologies, the cultural links with the home country are not as completely severed as in the past. Diasporas subsisted only when they were supported by a strong religious faith. Today, they can last for a long period even if there religious basis is weak. In many ways, a process of assimilation and integration develops, as in the past. It does not lead, however, to the easy fusion of the migrants in the host countries. They stick to their cultures because they wish to preserve their identities.

Cultural Competency

Cultural competency is the acceptance and respect for difference, a continuous self-assessment regarding culture, an attention to the dynamics of difference, the ongoing development of cultural knowledge, and the resources and flexibility within service models to meet the needs of minority populations. Cultural competency also as the integration and transformation of knowledge, information, and data about individuals and groups of people into specific clinical standards, skills, service approaches, techniques, and marketing programmes that match the individual's culture and increase the quality and appropriateness of health care and outcomes.

Cultural competency does not refer to the establishment or maintenance of diversity *per se*. Competency refers more explicitly to folkways, mores, traditions, customs, formal and informal helping networks, rituals, dialects, and so forth. In these areas, knowledge about various cultures and the development of specific skills and attitudes in providing services in a manner consistent with the client's needs are essential.

The cultural appropriateness of mental health services may be the most important factor in the accessibility of services by people of colour. Developing culturally sensitive practices can help reduce barriers to effective treatment utilisation. Rapport building is a critical component of competency development.

Ensuring the provision of culturally competent services to clients places a great deal of responsibility upon the mental health professional. In particular, there are a number of generally expected levels of knowledge, skills and attributes that are essential to providing culturally competent mental health services.

The most fundamental function of any therapeutic session is communication. In some European countires it is common for people to stand about three feet apart when having a personal conversation. In some other cultures, people may typically stand close, which may feel awkward to someone unfamiliar with this style. Individuals are encouraged to look each other directly in the eye and participate actively in feedback behaviours. In contrast, people from other backgrounds may show respect or deference by not engaging in eye contact or participating more passively in their body language. In some cultures people have come to expect a conversation to progress linearly, while in others it may be more natural for several people to be talking at once. Listening skills to deal with different turn-taking rules must be developed. Hand and arm gesturing can vary quite a bit in different cultural backgrounds.

The chief concern in communicating across cultures is ensuring that what one person intends is what the other hears. Additionally it is important to consider that communication consists of both verbal and non-verbal transmission of valuable information. It must also be recognised that more than one message is invariably being communicated at the same time. For communicating across languages, translation is a very difficult task. Problems are often associated with the interpreter's competence and translation skills, lack of familiarity with psychiatric terms, or with counselling knowledge and attitudes. Frequent errors include distortion, deletion, omission or blocking, exaggeration, incorrect translation, inappropriate cultural interpretation, or lack of translatable words or concepts.

Cultural Liberation

Cultural liberation is fostered by learning about other cultures and communicating with their members. It begins with the self-awareness to see one's own culture as such. In recognition of a pluralistic world, it develops by stages into biculturalism and multiculturalism. This is not a liberation from culture itself, as individuals would bring their culture(s) even into isolation from human contact. It is rather a liberation from identifying exclusively with one's own cultural entity and its members.

At the societal level, cultures cannot meet uncompromisingly anymore, the powerful or wealthy absorbing others into their own imperium. In a one-superpower world the danger is now unilateralism. Even world peace would meet with not only appreciation but also wariness. At a more deliberate pace and with a consultative approach, more lasting results can be achieved by multilateralism.

In a pluralistic world, different groups need to find a middle ground outside of any particular cultural framework, and to meet in mutual respect for there to be genuine communication. This cultural neutrality could be based on the recognition of universally human traits and aspirations. These aspirations are reflected in United Nations declarations such as those aiming to safeguard the global environment or linguistic and other human rights.

Another approach to a middle ground would be to synthesise elements of different cultures, even while each culture is preserved intact. International or multicultural organisations operate with parliamentary procedures that are culturally biased, such as Robert's Rules of Order. These procedures could be reformed, for example, to reflect effective Asian social practices that emphasise consultation, saving face and avoiding confrontations. Such reforms would represent biculturalism or multiculturalism instituted as an explicit policy, for the purpose of constructive collaboration among peoples of different cultures.

Multicultural organisations would be more democratic if their very procedures reflected the cultures involved, and international organisations could work better to make peace and solve problems facing the world. In multipolar global forums, each group will have to recognise the multiplicity of valid cultural viewpoints involved. Issues such as the rapid development of cities can be seen very differently depending upon whether the viewer is rich or poor, or upon cultural differences in the proxemics of personal space. In any international forum, while a *lingua franca* for discussions is needed, it is incumbent upon native speakers to see that the views of non-native speakers are registered.

Regional or economic blocs must not be over generalised into cultural monoliths, for example, lumping Asian cultures together under the rubric of Eastern thought, any more than one would mistake the European Community for a cultural monolith. Within Asia there are striking contrasts even between neighbouring cultures such as Korea, with its passions and bright colours displayed, and Japan, with its restrained subtlety and preference for subdued colours. Each country or ethnic group in Asia, as elsewhere, calls for a certain recognition of its cultural heritage.

So-called homogeneous societies such as Japan's, with relatively little cultural diversity, are prone to a sort of monoculturalism, a collective selfishness not essentially different from the individual kind. Whereas in so-called multicultural societies, such as Australia's, the mere juxtaposition of different cultures does not guarantee a relationship integrating them into a single society. There can also be a sort of competitive gridlock among constituent subcultures, as with Korean-Americans and Afro-Americans in Los Angeles in effect keeping each other down.

Every society could therefore do more to counter ethnocentrism with multiculturalism and internationalism. The world citizenship of individuals is hindered at this stage by nationalism, so grassroots initiatives must show the way to globalism. At face-to-face conferences, for example, American and Chinese scholars meet in friendship without waiting for their governments to reconcile. As people in most countries gain internet access, furthermore, discussion lists and other forms of computer-mediated communication are accelerating the direct dialogue between citizens of the world.

Turning to the individual level, the ethnocentric monoculturalist is a person who takes relative customs and beliefs for granted as absolutes. A certain religion may serve to maintain ethics among its community of believers, but trouble often occurs when other communities are expected to follow the same rules. Monoculturalists from different cultures can meet and similarly damn each other as barbarians, ironically. Monoculturalism is often simply the result of having little meaningful contact with people outside one's own culture. An individual can generally become aware of having a certain cultural background only through the comparison afforded by contacting members of a contrasting culture.

Even cross-cultural misunderstandings can have the value of demonstrating the limitations of mono-culturalism. Vastly outnumbered abroad, it is difficult to keep asserting that everyone else is doing things the wrong way. Then one may try approaching a problem differently, more like the other culture, and see surprisingly good results.

Adopting Asian-style politeness, gratitude, humility, a sense of reciprocity, becoming a good listener and more cooperative generally, may even make one more popular in a Western country. In any event, the facts of cross-cultural experience tend to lead one to see the previous monocultural *status quo* as narrow-mindedness, a handicap in self-development as well as in international interpersonal relations.

Cross-cultural encounters reveal that even common sensical assumptions differ radically among cultures. Foreigners in Japan, for example, face stark cultural differences which have nevertheless proven viable for the country itself. Just as individualism results in high productivity in the US, group-orientation does so in Japan. Each individual in Japan struggles to make the system work precisely because they are individuals and it is a hard job to adjust oneself to others.

Cultural differences are a matter of degree among universally human possibilities. Just like driving on the left side of the road, as in Japan, the system works because people agree to it. They agree that evasiveness or humble gestures defuse hostility, while self-justification is counter-productive, therefore social reality works that way in Japan. At some point a Westerner's native sense of certitude is liable to collide with another based on quite different assumptions, so certitude itself is called into question. This is a college of hard knocks, as adjusting to a contrasting and relatively impermeable culture like Japan's can constitute a stage even beyond mastering one of the world's most difficult languages.

Foreign language study must be recommended, because monolingualism is a gatekeeper of mono-culturalism. Foreign language education explicitly for intercultural communication, if unbiased and free of stereotyping, can open the door to cosmopolitanism.

Learning the local language is a more effective approach to intercultural communication. Intercultural training that advertises itself as an alternative to language learning can be justified for sojourners, but after several years in a country, not knowing its language becomes increasingly difficult to rationalise.

Some degree of bilinguality is instrumental to cultural liberation, but does not guarantee its seal. The respective cultural systems behind each language need to be held in mind for biculturalism and intercultural communication skills to develop. Then such communicative competence would have to be applied by the individual with equivalent ethical competence.

Now self-education and a degree of liberation need be no further than the nearest library or online computer. By living in different regions of a diverse country, an individual may be led by the facts of experience to transcend provincialism. By dint of study or introspection, it is possible to recognise the arbitrariness or relativity of one's culturally-based assumptions. In an ideal scenario, one would be able at will to take off one's culturally coloured glasses. But learning foreign languages generally certifies the effort needed to meet other cultures halfway.

East and West are beginning to unite within individuals, though the trend may not be recognised until the twenty-first century. This emergent social movement is largely thanks to the efforts of Asians and other non-native speakers of English who are adjusting themselves to core Western cultures. There is also a small but significant movement reciprocating from the side of English native speakers.

Communication based on mutual respect does not threaten the cultural heritage of either side, but adds knowledge and coping skills to the cultural repertoire of those involved. Clearly both sides have much to gain and mainly false pride to lose from intercultural alliances. It has proven possible to part with mutually exclusive national and cultural allegiances. Some of those born with dual nationality, for example, have had no difficulty identifying with both cultures. Biculturals can be both, and be cognitively enriched in the process.

Cross-cultural comparison and self-reflection, far from uprooting individuals culturally, shed light on their roots and the whole context of the field in which their roots are embedded. Without relinquishing cultural differences, the boundaries thereof can be transcended via awareness of cultures as such. Mentally healthy individuals can stand to be emancipated from the unconscious and hence involuntary processes of cultural identification that limit them and cut them off from the majority of humanity.

East-West studies of comparative culture may find a surprising number of traits to be universally human. It may even be found that the self-realisation process is universally human, but just manifests differently according to the culture. If this were recognised about the so-called collectivistic societies in Asia, and by Asian individuals themselves, great impetus would be given to grassroots globalism. Just as a seed is directed intelligently towards its potentiality as a full-grown tree, the self-realisation process could be considered universally human.

Educating Global Citizens

Nations throughout the world are faced with the problem of how to reflect the racial, ethnic, cultural and religious diversity within their societies while maintaining national unity. Increasing globalisation also challenging nationalism. The challenge of balancing diversity and unity is intensifying as democratic nations become more diversified and as racial and ethnic groups within these nations try to attain cultural, political and economic rights. The democratic ideologies within the major democratic nations and the wide gap between these ideals and realities were major factors that resulted in the rise of movements for cultural and economic rights in many democratic nations during the last four decades.

The democratic nations share a democratic ideal, a major tenet of which is that the state should protect human rights and promote equality and the inclusion of diverse groups into the mainstream society. These nations are also characterised by widespread inequality and by racial, ethnic, and class stratification. The discrepancy between democratic ideals and societal realities and the rising expectations of marginalised racial, ethnic, language and social-class groups created protest and revival movements within the Western democratic nations. These movements began with the civil rights movements in the United States during the 1960s and 1970s. The US civil rights movement echoed throughout the world.

Due to growing ethnic, cultural, racial, language and religious diversity throughout the world, citizenship education needs to be changed in substantial ways to prepare students to function effectively in the twenty-first century. Citizens in this century need the knowledge, attitudes, and skills required to function in their cultural communities and beyond their cultural borders. They should also be able and willing to participate in the construction of a national civic culture that is a moral and just community. The national community should embody democratic ideals and values, such as those articulated in the Universal Declaration of Human Rights, the Declaration of Independence, the Constitution, and the Bill of Rights. Students also need to acquire the knowledge and skills required to become effective citizens in the global community.

Citizenship education in the past, embraced an assimilationist ideology. In the United States, its aim was to educate students so they would fit into a mythical Anglo-Saxon Protestant conception of the 'good citizen'. Anglo conformity was the goal of citizenship education. One of its aims was to eradicate the community cultures and languages of students from diverse groups. One consequence of this assimilationist conception of citizenship education was that many students lost their first cultures, languages, and ethnic identities. Some students also became alienated from family and community. Another consequence was that many students became socially and politically alienated within the national civic culture.

Members of identifiable racial groups often became marginalised in both their community cultures and in the national civic culture because they could function effectively in neither. When they acquired the language and culture of the Anglo mainstream, they were often denied structural inclusion and full participation into the civic culture because of their racial characteristics.

Globalisation has made a deep imprint on the meaning of citizenship. Traditional definitions of citizenship are increasingly challenged by a new world order in which countries are compete against each other and multi-national companies and inter-government agencies have jurisdiction over local decisions. The draw of the dollar pulls people to migrate for short or long term as much as political unrest pushed people to migrate in years past. Globalisation has challenged the almighty power of the nation-state, and in doing so has shifted citizenship from being a passive "default" function of where one is born to an active descriptor of the various constituencies a given person can belong to. We moved from thinking of citizens as Indians, then hyphenated-Americans (Americans-Indians, German Indians, Irish-Indians, etc.), and increasingly as bi-nationals (dual passport holders).

The internet allows new migrants to maintain real time contact with their families and friends back home, eliminating the psychological break from the "old country" that has historically encouraged migrants to establish a stronger sense of permanency. Migrants such as the Chinese leaving Hong Kong recently exercised a certain level of choice in where to go and invest their capital, making governments a player in the marketplace of attracting migrants. Citizenship is becoming as much a chosen identity as much as a birthright.

Globalisation has put economic activity on par with political engagement in shaping global markets and foreign policy. The world is becoming more and more economically interdependent, and there is an increasing need to think about "economic citizenship" as a growing element to citizenship in the modern world. By defining "economic citizenship" as involving the rights and responsibilities of living in an economic community, significant thought must be given to the responsibilities that this would entail. Since the capitalist economic model runs on individual choice and offers little opportunity for collective action, the majority of people acting in the economy think seldom about their role as an "economic citizen" and do little to exercise the limited amount of responsibility they have in their control.

"Citizenship" has historically described the rights and duties of being a member of a political community, not an economic one. An analysis of citizenship as including the responsibilities of individuals living in an economic community must address the distinct jurisdictions in which these people are operating and the uncoupling of right and responsibilities that results from this. A Mexican living in Seattle bears rights that come from living in a liberal Western democracy, but those rights are not matched with responsibilities within the jurisdiction of Seattle. His responsibilities most likely still live in Mexico, giving him a personal investment not where he lives but where he comes from.

The Hong Kong Chinese living in Vancouver, British Columbia, act similarly as "economic citizens" with de-linked rights and responsibilities: they have rights living in Canada, but their global identity leads them to invest themselves in their familial and cultural responsibilities rather than possible civic responsibilities. Many educators will attest to the difficulty of getting the parents of recently-arrived immigrant students involved in their child's school, both as a factor of cultural differences and because of financial responsibilities that have them working two and three jobs to support their family both here and in their country of origin.

A last element of "economic citizenship" worth touching upon because of its relevance to schools is the often conflictual relationship between those who identify themselves in some way as actors in a global economy and those who do not. Amy Chua, author of *World on Fire*, wrote in a recent New York *Times* opinion piece that a paradox of globalisation results when laissez-faire capitalism is combined with free elections in such a way that economic minorities are able to disrupt a country's power structure.

In countries around the world, "market dominant minorities" such as the Chinese in Canada conflict with the democratic majority, sometimes resulting in disastrous outcomes. While the extreme versions of this conflict are limited to developing nations already unstable in the world economy, the significance of the chasm between the globally-prepared citizens being churned out of the best schools and the majority of other students who do not have such global awakenings is important as we rethink the educational system.

Culture and citizenship have an iterative relationship: elements of a dominant culture are reflected in their legal and cultural citizenship practices, and citizenship standards over time influence a society's culture. A humanitarian interest in protecting members of its former colonies, for example, led the United Kingdom to grant citizenship to a high numbers of Indians, who in turn had an influence on British culture. It might be argued that the UK granted legal citizenship to Indians but not necessarily cultural citizenship, with many British subjects castigating Indian migrants as the source of all bad in British society.

The articulation of the relationship between culture and citizenship is important, however, because it raises the issue of whether the culture indoctrinated in public policy and governing institutions reflects the culture of those individuals presently citizens in a given place. The introduction of economics as an influence equal to politics in the new world order challenges the tradition relationship between culture and citizenship.

Multiculturalism encouraged an interest in and respect for the many cultures within society, but the core rights and responsibilities of living in the United States were uniformly agreed upon, more or less, by immigrant and native born alike. If citizenship is a subset of culture, a society with many cultures will reflect many varying definitions of citizenship. Globalisation is eroding the potential for one, unifying culture rooted in a compelling national narrative. While most people can continue to agree at some level on the rights that society should extend to all members, a set of mutually agreed upon responsibilities comes less easily because of the influences of the culture of individuals with economic responsibilities outside the nation.

Transformation of Citizenship Education

Citizenship education is transforming in the twenty-first century. Several worldwide developments make a new conception of citizenship education an imperative. They include the deepening ethnic texture of nations such as the United States, Canada, Australia, Germany, the United Kingdom, and Japan. The large influx of immigrants who are now settling in nations throughout the world, the continuing existence of institutional racism and discrimination in various nations, and the widening gap between rich and poor nations also make the reform of citizenship education an imperative.

Schools are the primary institutions engaged in the business of educating citizens. They are being called upon to play a greater role in preparing the young people to be globally-minded citizens. The 'melting pot' model of the past is being challenged because of globalisation and divided economic loyalties, and a new definition of citizenship for the new world order will better serve all students as they look to join a world that extends well beyond the national borders.

Since schools are tasked with the production of citizens, a redefinition of citizenship would serve to refocus what is offered within the schools. Some of the most important elements include:

i) Comprehensive knowledge about world political systems
ii) Comprehensive knowledge about world economic systems
iii) Critical thinking skills to analyse issues that span political-economic lines
iii) Cross-cultural communication skills
iv) Opportunities to practise engagement as "active" citizen
v) Opportunities to build empathy for others
vi) Forums that serve as the "public sphere"

As the boundaries for learning become more and more remote, increased attention needs to be paid to the relevance of learning for students. Now that economics and politics stand on equal footing and are indecipherably intermingled, educating the young people for global citizenship has become more difficult, and the relevance of this increased amount of necessary knowledge is not always obvious. This is particularly key for students who are not afforded the opportunities from the outset to see the world through a global lens. As some students see the relevance and others do not, the chasm between the two groups could result in effects detrimental to society as a whole.

Global education, therefore must shift to help students personalise the world and internalise their connection to people living in worlds far away. The challenge of integrating "global studies" themes with an indepth knowledge of countries and cultures enriched by the diverse voices and stories that capture the human experience can overwhelm the most experienced teacher. Diverse and interdependent community organisations can serve as important partners to teachers as they model a diverse and interdependent world in their classroom. Robust content knowledge requires that students learn the indepth histories of other countries.

Rather than survey courses that introduce students briefly to the most superficial differences among many countries, a new global curriculum must seek to build an understanding of interdependence that can only be achieved by probing deeply into a few countries. This requires that students develop an understanding of major themes evolving in the world today and then be able to analyse how these themes play out in different areas of the world with similar results, mediated by culture and geography. An appreciation for multiculturalism is then achieved because students gain an indepth understanding of the early history and philosophies of a culture that they can then apply to other cultures. In terms of the ubiquitous "cultural iceberg" used by educators to demonstrate culture, students learn about the ninety-percent of a culture that exists beneath the surface, thereby gaining new skills in understanding all cultures. Any model of a global curriculum that puts understanding perspectives and authentic application at its core is a curriculum that cannot be taught in isolation. It demands that teachers and schools model the level of involvement and curiosity. The new world order is being similar to the world wide web, with nodes of actors independently interconnected, bringing great advantage to those who are connected. Classrooms, similarly, are greatly enriched when they are defined not by the four walls that enclose them but as a nexus of community resources that teachers can draw upon to build understanding of the greater world.

Citizens in a diverse democratic society should be able to maintain attachments to their cultural communities as well as participate effectively in the shared national culture. Unity without diversity results in cultural repression and hegemony. Diversity without unity leads to balkanisation and the fracturing of the nation-state.

Diversity and unity should coexist in a delicate balance in a democratic multicultural nation-state. The attainment of the balance that is needed between diversity and unity is an ongoing process and ideal that is never fully attained. It is essential that both mainstream groups and groups on the margins of society participate in the formulation of societal goals related to diversity and unity. Both groups should also participate in action to attain these goals. Deliberation and the sharing of power by mainstream and marginalised groups are essential for the construction and perpetuation of a just, moral, and participatory democratic nation-state in a culturally diverse society.

The twenty-first century needs multicultural citizenship which recognises and legitimises the right and need of citizens to maintain commitments both to their cultural communities and to the national civic culture. Only when the national civic culture is transformed in ways that reflect and give voice to the diverse ethnic, racial, language, and religious communities that constitute it will it be viewed as legitimate by all of its citizens. Only then can they develop clarified commitments to the nation-state and its ideals.

Citizenship education should help students to develop thoughtful and clarified identifications with their cultural communities and their nation-states. It should also help them to develop clarified global identifications and deep understandings of their roles in the world community. Students need to understand how life in their cultural communities and nations influences other nations and the cogent influence that international events have on their daily lives. Global education should have as major goals helping students to develop understandings of the interdependence among nations in the world today, clarified attitudes toward other nations, and reflective identifications with the world community.

Non-reflective and unexamined cultural attachments may prevent the development of a cohesive nation with clearly defined national goals and policies. Blind nationalism will prevent students from developing reflective and positive global identifications. In most nations, nationalism and national attachments are strong and tenacious. An important aim of citizenship education should be to help students develop global identifications and a deep understanding of the need to take action as citizens of the global community to help solve the world's difficult global problems, such as conflict and war, the AIDS/HIV epidemic, global warming, and world poverty.

Cultural, national, and global experiences and identifications are interactive and interrelated in a dynamic way. Students should develop a delicate balance of cultural, national, and global identifications. A nation-state that alienates and does not structurally include all cultural groups into the national culture runs the risk of creating alienation and causing groups to focus on specific concerns and issues rather than on the overarching goals and policies of the nation-state. To develop reflective cultural, national and global identifications, students must acquire the knowledge, attitudes and skills needed to function within and across diverse racial, ethnic, cultural, language and religious groups.

UNESCO Universal Declaration on Cultural Diversity

The UNESCO Universal Declaration on Cultural Diversity was adopted by the 31st Session of the General Conference of UNESCO, paris, 2 November, 2001.

The General Committee,

Committed to the full implementation of the human rights and fundamental freedoms proclaimed in the Universal Declaration of Human Rights and other universally recognised legal instruments, such as the two International Covenants of 1966 relating respectively to civil and political rights and to economic, social and cultural rights,

Recalling that the Preamble to the Constitution of UNESCO affirms "that the wide diffusion of culture, and the education of humanity for justice and liberty and peace are indispensable to the dignity of man and constitute a sacred duty which all the nations must fulfil in a spirit of mutual assistance and concern",

Further recalling Article I of the Constitution, which assigns to UNESCO among other purposes that of recommending "such international agreements as may be necessary to promote the free flow of ideas by word and image",

Referring to the provisions relating to cultural diversity and the exercise of cultural rights in the international instruments enacted by UNESCO,

Reaffirming that culture should be regarded as the set of distinctive spiritual, material, intellectual and emotional features of society or a social group, and that it encompasses, in addition to art and literature, lifestyles, ways of living together, value systems, traditions and beliefs,

Noting that culture is at the heart of contemporary debates about identity, social cohesion, and the development of a knowledge-based economy,

Affirming that respect for the diversity of cultures, tolerance, dialogue and cooperation, in a climate of mutual trust and understanding are among the best guarantees of international peace and security,

Aspiring to greater solidarity on the basis of recognition of cultural diversity, of awareness of the unity of humankind, and of the development of intercultural exchanges,

Considering that the process of globalisation, facilitated by the rapid development of new information and communication technologies, though representing a challenge for cultural diversity, creates the conditions for renewed dialogue among cultures and civilisations,

Aware of the specific mandate which has been entrusted to UNESCO, within the United Nations system, to ensure the preservation and promotion of the fruitful diversity of cultures, *Proclaims* the following principles and adopts the present Declaration:

Identinty Diversity and Pluralism

Article 1. Cultural Diversity: The Common Heritage of Humanity

Culture takes diverse forms across time and space. This diversity is embodied in the uniqueness and plurality of the identities of the groups and societies making up humankind. As a source of exchange, innovation and creativity, cultural diversity is as necessary for humankind as biodiversity is for nature. In this sense, it is the common heritage of humanity and should be recognised and affirmed for the benefit of present and future generations.

Article 2. From Cultural Diversity to Cultural Pluralism

In this increasingly diverse societies, it is essential to ensure harmonious interaction among people and groups with plural, varied and dynamic cultural identities as well as their willingness to live together. Policies for the inclusion and participation of all citizens are guarantees of social cohesion, the vitality of civil society and peace. Thus defined, cultural pluralism gives policy expression to the reality of cultural diversity. Indissociable from a democratic framework, cultural pluralism is conducive to cultural exchange and to the flourishing of creative capacities that sustain public life.

Article 3. Cultural Diversity as a Factor in Development

Cultural diversity widens the range of options open to everyone; it is one of the roots of development, understood not simply in terms of economic growth, but also as a means to achieve a more satisfactory intellectual, emotional, moral and spiritual existence.

Cultural Diversity and Human Rights

Article 4. Human Rights as Guarantees of Cultural Diversity

The defence of cultural diversity is an ethical imperative, inseparable from respect for human dignity. It implies a commitment to human rights and fundamental freedoms, in particular the rights of persons belonging to minorities and those of indigenous peoples. No one may invoke cultural diversity to infringe upon human rights guaranteed by international law, nor to limit their scope.

Article 5. Cultural Rights as an Enabling Environment for Cultural Diversity

Cultural rights are an integral part of human rights, which are universal, indivisible and interdependent. The flourishing of creative diversity requires the full implementation of cultural rights as defined in Article 27 of the Universal Declaration of Human Rights and in Articles 13 and 15 of the International Covenant on Economic, Social and Cultural Rights. All persons have therefore the right to express themselves and to create and disseminate their work in the language of their choice, and particularly in their mother tongue; all persons are entitled to quality education and training that fully respect their cultural identity; and all persons have the right to participate in the cultural life of their choice and conduct their own cultural practices, subject to respect for human rights and fundamental freedoms.

Article 6. Towards Access for all to Cultural Diversity

While ensuring the free flow of ideas by word and image care should be exercised that all cultures can express themselves and make themselves known. Freedom of expression, media pluralism, multilingualism, equal access to art and to scientific and technological knowledge, including in digital form, and the possibility for all cultures to have access to the means of expression and dissemination are the guarantees of cultural diversity.

Cultural Diversity and Creativity

Article 7. Cultural Heritage as the Wellspring of Creativity

Creation draws on the roots of cultural tradition, but flourishes in contact with other cultures. For this reason, heritage in all its forms must be preserved, enhanced and handed on to future generations as a record of human experience and aspirations, so as to foster creativity in all its diversity and to inspire genuine dialogue among cultures.

Article 8. Cultural Goods and Services: Commodities of a Unique kind

In the face of present-day economic and technological change, opening up vast prospects for creation and innovation, particular attention must be paid to the diversity of the supply of creative work, to due recognition of the rights of authors and artists and to the specificity of cultural goods and services which, as vectors of identity, values and meaning, must not be treated as mere commodities or consumer goods.

Article 9. Cultural Policies as Catalysts of Creativity

While ensuring the free circulation of ideas and works, cultural policies must create conditions conducive to the production and dissemination of diversified cultural goods and services through cultural industries that have the means to assert themselves at the local and global level. It is for each State, with due regard to its international obligations, to define its cultural policy and to implement it through the means it considers fit, whether by operational support or appropriate regulations.

Cultural Diversity and International Solidiarity

Article 10. Strengthening Capacities for Creation and Dissemination Worldwide

In the face of current imbalances in flows and exchanges of cultural goods and services at the global level, it is necessary to reinforce international cooperation and solidarity aimed at enabling all countries, especially developing countries and countries in transition, to establish cultural industries that are viable and competitive at national and international level.

Article 11. Building Partnerships among the Public Sector, the Private Sector and Civil Society

Market forces alone cannot guarantee the preservation and promotion of cultural diversity, which is the key to sustainable human development. From this perspective, the pre-eminence of public policy, in partnership with the private sector and civil society, must be reaffirmed.

Article 12. The Role of UNESCO

UNESCO, by virtue of its mandate and functions, has the responsibility to:

a) Promote the incorporation of the principles set out in the present Declaration into the development strategies drawn up within the various inter-governmental bodies;
b) Serve as a reference point and a forum where States, international governmental and non-governmental organisations, civil society and the private sector may join together in elaborating concepts, objectives and policies in favour of cultural diversity;

c) Pursue its activities in standard-setting, awareness-raising and capacity-building in the areas related to the present Declaration within its fields of competence;

d) Facilitate the implementation of the Action Plan, the main lines of which are appended to the present Declaration.

Main Lines of an Action Plan for the Implementation of the UNESCO Universal Declaration on Cultural Diversity

The Member-States commit themselves to taking appropriate steps to disseminate widely the "UNESCO Universal Declaration on Cultural Diversity" and to encourage its effective application, in particular by cooperating with a view to achieving the following objectives:

1. Deepening the international debate on questions relating to cultural diversity, particularly in respect of its links with development and its impact on policy making, at both the national and the international levels; taking forward notably consideration of the advisability of an international legal instrument on cultural diversity.
2. Advancing in the definition of principles, standards and practices, on both the national and the international levels, as well as of awareness-raising modalities and patterns of cooperation, that are most conducive to the safeguarding and promotion of cultural diversity.
3. Fostering the exchange of knowledge and best practices in regard to cultural pluralism with a view to facilitating, in diversified societies, the inclusion and participation of persons and groups from varied cultural backgrounds.
4. Making further headway in understanding and clarifying the content of cultural rights as an integral part of human rights.

5. Safeguarding the linguistic heritage of humanity and giving support to expression, creation and dissemination in the greatest possible number of languages.
6. Encouraging linguistic diversity — while respecting the mother tongue — at all levels of education, wherever possible, and fostering the learning of several languages from the earliest age.
7. Promoting through education an awareness of the positive value of cultural diversity and improving to this end both curriculum design and teacher education.
8. Incorporating, where appropriate, traditional pedagogies into the education process with a view to preserving and making full use of culturally appropriate methods of communication and transmission of knowledge.
9. Encouraging "digital literacy" and ensuring greater mastery of the new information and communication technologies, which should be seen both as educational discipline and as pedagogical tools capable of enhancing the effectiveness of educational services.
10. Promoting linguistic diversity in cyberspace and encouraging universal access through the global network to all information in the public domain.
11. Countering the digital divide, in close cooperation in relevant United Nations system organisations, by fostering access by the developing countries to the new technologies, by helping them to master information technologies and by facilitating the digital dissemination of endogenous cultural products and access by those countries to the educational, cultural and scientific digital resources available worldwide.
12. Encouraging the production, safeguarding and dissemination of diversified contents in the media and global information networks and, to that end, promoting the role of public radio and television services in the development of audiovisual productions

of good quality, in particular by fostering the establishment of cooperative mechanisms to facilitate their distribution.

13. Formulating policies and strategies for the preservation and enhancement of the cultural and natural heritage, notably the oral and intangible cultural heritage, and combating illicit traffic in cultural goods and services.
14. Respecting and protecting traditional knowledge, in particular that of indigenous peoples; recognising the contribution of traditional knowledge, particularly with regard to environmental protection and the management of natural resources, and fostering synergies between modern science and local knowledge.
15. Fostering the mobility of creators, artists, researchers, scientists and intellectuals and the development of international research programmes and partnerships, while striving to preserve and enhance the creative capacity of developing countries and countries in transition.
16. Ensuring protection of copyright and related rights in the interest of the development of the Member-States recommend contemporary creativity and fair remuneration for creative work, while at the same time upholding a public right of access to culture, in accordance with Article 27 of the Universal Declaration of Human Rights.
17. Assisting in the emergence or consolidation of cultural industries in the developing countries and countries in transition and, to this end, cooperating in the development of the necessary infrastructures and skills, fostering the emergence of viable local markets, and facilitating access for the cultural products of those countries to the global market and international distribution networks.
18. Developing cultural policies, including operational support arrangements and/or appropriate regulatory

frameworks, designed to promote the principles enshrined in this Declaration, in accordance with the international obligations incumbent upon each State.

19. Involving all sectors of civil society closely in framing of public policies aimed at safeguarding and promoting cultural diversity.
20. Recognizing and encouraging the contribution that the private sector can make to enhancing cultural diversity and facilitating, to that end, the establishment of forums for dialogue between the public sector and the private sector.

The Member-States recommend that the Director-General take the objectives set forth in this Action Plan into account in the implementation of UNESCO's programmes and communicate it to institutions of the United Nations system and to other inter-governmental and non-governmental organisations concerned with a view to enhancing the synergy of actions in favour of cultural diversity.

References

Banks, J. A. , *Educating Citizens in a Multicultural Society*, New York: Teachers College Press,1997.

______________ *Diversity and Citizenship Education: Global Perspectives*, San Francisco: Jossey-Bass, 2003.

______________ , Cookson, Peter., Gay, Geneva., Hawley, Willis. D., Irvine, Jacqueline. J., Nieto, Sonia., Schofield, Janet W. and Stephan, Walter. G. , *Diversity within Unity: Essential Principles for Teaching and Learning in a Multicultural Society*, Seattle: Center for Multicultural Education, University of Washington, 2001.

Castles, Stephen and Davidson, Alastair, *Citizenship and Migration: Globalisation and the Politics of Belonging*, New York: The Guilford Press, 2000.

Davis, King, "Race, Health Status, and Managed Care", in Epstein, Len and Brisbane, Francis (eds.), *Cultural Competence Series*, Rockville, MD: Center for Substance Abuse Prevention, 1997.

Ichilov, Orit (ed.), *Citizenship and Citizenship Education in a Changing World*, London: The Woburn Press, 1998.

Kymlicka, Will Multicultural Citizenship: A Liberal Theory of Minority Rights, New York: Oxford University Press, 1995.

Lynch, James, *Education for Citizenship in a multicultural society*, London/New York, Cassell, 1992.

Parker, W. C., *Teaching Democracy: Unity and Diversity in Public Life*, New York: Teachers College Press, 2003.

5

Education in a Multilingual World

In many countries, education takes place in multilingual contexts. Most plurilingual societies have developed an ethos which balances and respects the use different languages in daily life. From the perspective of these societies and of the language communities themselves, multilingualism is more a way of life than a problem to be solved. These complex realities and provide equality education which takes into consideration learners' needs, whilst balancing these at the same time with social, cultural and political demands.

Over 70 per cent of all languages in the world are found in just 20 nation states, among them some of the poorest countries the world. Bilingualism and multilingualism, that is, the use of more than one language in daily life, linguistically diverse contexts cover a range of scenarios. The concept of linguistic diversity itself is relative, however, and is usually measured in terms of national boundaries, giving some languages the status of majority language and others that of minority language according to specific national contexts.

However, most of the world's languages, including sign languages for the deaf and braille for the blind, are minority languages in any national context. Nevertheless, the term 'minority' is often ambiguous and may be interpreted differently in distinct contexts because it may have both numerical and social or political dimensions. In some cases it may be simply used as a euphemism for non-elite or subordinate groups, whether they constitute a numerical majority or minority in relation to some other group that is politically and socially dominant.

The majority of countries in the world are monolingual nation states in the sense of recognising, *de jure* or *de facto*, only one official language for government and legal purposes. That is not to say that they are not bilingualor multilingual societies, but rather that while there may be many languages widely used in a country these do not necessarily have the legal authority of an official language.

In many countries that were previously under colonial regimes, the official language tends to be the language of the former colonisers. In addition to official languages, several countries recognise national languages, which may be compulsory in education. The choice of language in the educational system confers a power and prestige through its use in formal instruction. Not only is there a symbolic aspect, referring to status and visibility, but also a conceptual aspect referring to shared values and world view expressed through and in that language.

The language of instruction in or out of school refers to the language used for teaching the basic curriculum of the educational system. The choice of the language or indeed the languages of instruction is a recurrent challenge in the development of quality education. While some countries opt for one language of instruction, often the official or majority language, others have chosen to use educational strategies that give national or local languages an important place in schooling.

'Mother tongue' may also be referred to as 'primary' or 'first language'. The term 'mother tongue' is commonly used in policy statements and in the general discourse on educational issues. A child's earliest first-hand experiences in native speech do not necessarily correspond to the formal school version of the so-called mother tongue. It is an obvious yet not generally recognised truism that learning in a language which is not one's own provides a double set of challenges, not only is there the challenge of learning a new language but also that of learning new knowledge contained in that language.

Gender considerations cross-cut these situations of educational risk, for girls and women may be in a particularly disadvantaged position. In most traditional societies, it is the girls and women who tend to be monolingual, being less exposed either through schooling, salaried labour, or migration to the national language, than their sons, brothers or husbands.

Language is also a fundamental attribute of cultural identity and empowerment, both for the individual and the group. Respect for the languages of persons belonging to different linguistic communities therefore is essential to peaceful cohabitation. This applies both to majority groups, to minorities and to indigenous peoples. Claims for language are among the first rights that minorities have voiced when there have been situations of political change and evolution. Such claims for linguistic rights range from the official and legal status of the minority and indigenous language, to language teaching and use in schools and other institutions, as well as in the media.

In school, the language of instruction is the medium of communication for the transmission of knowledge. This is different from language teaching itself where the grammar, vocabulary, and the written and the oral forms of a language constitute a specific curriculum for the acquisition of a second language other than the mother tongue. Learning another language opens up access to other value systems and ways of interpreting the world, encouraging inter-cultural understanding and helping reduce xenophobia. This applies equally to minority and majority language speakers. The way languages are taught is constantly changing, and may vary considerably from one country to another or even within the same country.

As one of the fundamental standard-setting instruments, the Universal Declaration of Human Rights, proclaimed in 1948, lays down the basic principle against discrimination on the grounds of language: 'Article 2.: Every one is entitled to all rights and freedoms set forth in this Declaration, without distinction of any kind, such as... language'. The rights of persons belonging to minorities are furthermore established by the 1966 International Covenant on Civil and Political Rights and the 1992 Declaration on the Rights of Persons belonging to National or Ethnic, Religious and Linguistic Minorities.

Whereas Article 27 of the International Covenant refers more generally to the right of persons belonging to minorities' to use their own language ... in community with the other members of their group', the Declaration is of explicit relevance to the language issue in the field of education as it formulates in Article 4 that persons belonging to minorities should have adequate opportunities 'to learn their mothertongue or to have instruction in their mother tongue' and that measures should be taken 'in order to encourage knowledge of the ... language and culture of the minorities'.

Article 28 requires that 'children belonging to the peoples concerned shall, wherever practicable, be taught to read and write in their own indigenous language or in the language most commonly used by the group to which they belong' and that 'adequate measures shall be taken to ensure that these peoples have the opportunity to attain fluency in the national language or in one of the official languages of the country'. The Article provides at the same time that 'measures shall be taken to preserve and promote the development and practice of the indigenous languages of the peoples concerned'.

The 1990 International Convention on the Protection of the Rights of All Migrant Workers and Members of Their Families puts forth that 'States of employment shall pursue a policy ... aimed at facilitating the integration of children of migrant workers in the local school system, particularly in respect of teaching them the local language', and 'the teaching of their mother tongue and culture'; they may furthermore' provide special schemes of education in the mother tongue of children of migrant workers' (Article 45).

The 1960 Convention against Discrimination in Education lays down the educational rights of persons belonging to minorities. Article 5 has a particular relevance to the language issue as the respective roles of the mother tongue and of the majority language are defined: 'the members of national minorities to carry on their own educational activities, including... the use or the teaching of their own language, provided... that this right is not exercised in a manner which prevents the members of these minorities from understanding the culture and language of the community as a whole and from participating in its activities'.

The 1995 Declaration and Integrated Framework of Action on Education for Peace, Human Rights and Democracy promotes foreign language learning (Article 19) and the 'respect for the educational rights of persons belonging to ... minorities, as well as indigenous peoples' in order to foster understanding between communities and nations (Article 11), the Universal Declaration on Cultural Diversity, adopted in 2001, likewise touches upon the importance of languages for the promotion of cultural diversity.

Article 6 of the Action Plan for the implementation of the Declaration defines the role that languages should play in the field of education including respect for the mother tongue, linguistic diversity at all levels of education and the promotion of multilingualism from an early age.

In recenty years, many of the world summits held under the auspices of the United Nations and following an intergovernmental logic have noted the core importance of languages. A case in point is the Beijing Declaration and Platform for Action, adopted in 1995 at the Fourth World Conference on Women affirms the principle of equal access to education which has to be achieved through the elimination of 'discrimination in education at all levels on the basis of ... language.'

Mother tongue instruction appears to be a recurrent issue. The Delhi Declaration and Framework for Action, adopted in 1993 at the Education for All Summit, takes an explicit stand on the issue of mother tongue instruction by supporting 'initial instruction in the mother tongue, even if it may in some cases be necessary for the students to subsequently master a national language or other language of wider usage if they are to participate effectively in the broader society of which they are part.'

The need to acknowledge 'the essential role of the mother tongue for initial instruction' is also formulated in the 1996 Amman Affirmation, the final communiqué of the Mid-Decade Meeting of the International Consultative Forum on Education for All. The 1997 Hamburg Declaration on Adult Learning, adopted at the Fifth International Conference on Adult Education, states the importance of the issue for minority groups and indigenous peoples and proposes that 'the right to learn in the mother tongue should be respected and implemented' (Article 15).

The Vienna Declaration and Programme of Action adopted by the World Conference on Human Rights (1993) provides more generally in section I, paragraph 19 that the 'persons belonging to minorities have the right... to use their own language in private and in public, freely and without interference or any form of discrimination'. The 1998 World Declaration on Higher Education for the Twenty-first Century: Vision and Action puts forth the importance of multilingualism in higher education: in order to encourage international understanding, 'the practice of multilingualism, faculty and student exchange programmes should be an integral part of all higher education systems' (Article 15).

In the field of language and education, the recent reports and recommendations of the International Conference on Education (ICE) have emphasised the importance of: mother tongue instruction at the beginning of formal education for pedagogical, social and cultural considerations; multilingual education with a view to the preservation of cultural identities and the promotion of mobility and dialogue; foreign language learning as part of an intercultural education aiming at the promotion of understanding between communities and between nations.

Educating Language Minority Students

Differences in cultures are more substantial than whether members of a community eat white bread, corn pone, or tortillas. The behaviour of people varies, and the beliefs, values, and assumptions that underlie behaviour differ as well. Culture influences both behaviour and the psychological processes on which it rests. Culture forms a prism through which members of a group see the world and create shared meanings. And a group's culture is reflected by the group's language. Child development follows a pattern similar to that of culture.

Major structural changes in children, such as language learning, arise from the interaction of biology and experience. Such changes are remarkably similar in kind and sequence among cultural groups. But the knowledge and skills—the cultural learning—the child acquires at various ages depend on the child's family and community. Learning a primary language is a developmental milestone. However, which language a child learns and the uses to which that language is put are determined by the culture.

As the ideas from a child's social world are brought to bear through the guidance of the older members of the community, children come to share meanings with their elders. Classroom discourse presents children with the challenge of learning new rules for communication. The use of formal language, teacher control of verbal exchanges, question-and-answer formats, and references to increasingly abstract ideas characterise the classroom environment. To the extent that these new rules overlap with those that children have already learned, classroom communication is made easier.

Teachers facing the challenge of teaching children from different cultural communities are hard-pressed to decide what constitutes an appropriate curriculum. Cultural diversity makes it hard for teachers to assess each child's developmental status, find common educational experiences to promote growth, and measure the achievement of educational objectives. Teachers need to learn to recognise developmentally equivalent patterns of behaviour.

Before children come to school, they have all learned many of the same things, such as a primary language and communication styles. Although these developmental accomplishments may look different, they are developmentally equivalent. When a child does not respond to the social and cognitive expectations of the school, the teacher should look for a developmentally equivalent task to which the child will respond. Teachers with doubts about the development of culturally different children should assume that the children are normal and look at them again, recognising that their own vision may be clouded by cultural myopia.

Teachers need to begin instruction with interactive styles and content that is familiar to the children. Whether this entails speaking in the child's primary language, using culturally appropriate styles of address, or relying on patterns of management familiar to the children, the purpose is to establish a basis for communication. While fluency in a child's primary language may not be possible for many teachers, they can none the less become more adept at planning and implementing a culturally sensitive curriculum.

Such a curriculum encompasses more than tasting parties, ethnic costumes, and shopworn introductions to practices of people from different nations or racial groups. In order to teach such a curriculum, teachers must come to grips with their own ethnocentricity. School learning is most likely to occur when family values reinforce school expectations. Parents and other community members must view school achievement as a desirable and attainable goal if children are to build it into their sense of self. Interpreting the school's agenda for parents is one of the most important tasks for teachers.

When differences exist between the cultural patterns of the home and community and those of the school, teachers must deal with these discrepancies directly. Teachers and children must create shared understandings and new contexts that give meaning to the knowledge and skills being taught. Learning mediated by teachers who are affectionate, interested, and responsive has greater sticking power than learning mediated by an adult who is perceived as impersonal and distant.

Assessment of learning outcomes presents a formidable problem when children misunderstand the teacher's requests for information or demonstrations of knowledge and skills. Formal assessment should be delayed until teachers and children have built a set of new meanings. A developmentally appropriate curriculum can never be standardised in a multicultural community. But thoughtful teachers can use principles of child development to make the new context of school meaningful and to safeguard the self-confidence of children.

Reforms in School Environment

Change is a constant for schools. Many factors contribute to a continuous modification of schools' missions and services: demographic shifts; new policy, curricula, and procedures created at the district and state levels; internal conditions and decisions by administrators, teachers, and students. However, the current reform movement promises to surpass previous change efforts by far.

Encompassing a variety of initiatives for fundamental change in the way schools function to promote student success, this movement promises to affect everyone—students and teachers, principals and superintendents, parents and employers. Like earlier drives for reform, the current one aims to improve students' academic achievement. The focus is on rethinking and restructuring schools to serve all students well.

Curriculum and instruction are being modified to challenge and engage all students and to articulate programmes across grade levels. Central to this reform is the involvement of staff members in decisionmaking. This entails changing the way practitioners relate to each other, to administrators, to students, and to parents. Traditional hierarchical structures are giving way to more collaborative structures. The goal is to re-conceptualise and renew the school's total operation from within so that reform is tailored to local conditions and teachers are committed to what they have helped to craft.

Changing School Leadership

The strong leadership remains crucial to the change process. As a culturally and linguistically diverse school works collaboratively to refine a shared vision of excellent schooling and an educational programme that reflects it, the principal must continually advocate for the inclusion of English language learners. By explicitly keeping language and culture on the reform agenda and insisting that every teacher participate in the school's continuous improvement process, the principal can ensure sustained attention to these students.

Reforming a school usually requires that the whole staff or significant groups within it take stock of their practices and devise new directions. This may mean modifying traditional beliefs and practices to respond more accurately to students' learning needs. One useful mechanism for change is inquiry groups, in which teachers raise questions about students' success in their school, gather and analyse data, and plan responses.

Teachers' inquiry may also focus on the "puzzlements" that teachers may experience when they do not share linguistic and cultural backgrounds with their students. Current views of reform also emphasise strengthening and transforming school relationships with parents and the community to make them more collaborative. Regardless of income or level of education, parents can support children's education, for example, by reading with them and talking about the text in the native language or in English. Even when parents' own level of literacy is low, they support their children's education when they encourage an inquiry approach to learning in the home.

Schools need to develop partnerships with parents that allow them to identify and validate such parental contributions to the shared task of educating students. Similarly, the potential benefit of collaboration among culturally diverse communities and schools has not yet been fully realised. Social service organisations can be useful to both families and schools, offering health services to families of language minority students, for example, and organising meetings where parents and educators exchange information.

Culturally Diverse Parents

Teachers and other professionals providing education-related services to exceptional children from different cultural backgrounds need to be aware of unique perspectives or communication styles common to those cultures. The ways people deal with feelings—especially disappointment, anxiety, fear, embarrassment, and anger—vary considerably, and often it is not easy to discern how parents are reacting to the realisation that their child has a disability. To facilitate communication, educators should use the following guidelines:

i) Send messages home in the parent's native language.

ii) Use an appropriate reading level.

iii) Listen to messages being returned.

Courtesy, sincerity, and ample opportunity and time to convey concerns can promote communication with and participation by parents from different cultural backgrounds. Educators need to listen with empathy and realise that parents can change from feelings of trust to scepticism or curiosity as their understanding of programmes and policies increases. It is important to realise that this reaction is normal and that parents may feel hostile or desperate as they attempt to sort out facts from their fundamental beliefs about education.

In communicating with families from different cultural groups, educators should keep in mind their diverse cultural styles. There is no one set of characteristics that can be ascribed to all members of any ethnic group. Instead, the cultural traits of individuals range from those traditionally attributed to the ethnic group to those that are descriptive of a person who has been totally assimilated into the majority culture.

People from different cultures use, value, and share space differently. In some cultures it is considered appropriate for people to stand very close to each other while talking, whereas in other cultures people like to keep farther apart. Rules for touching others vary from culture to culture. Some cultures, however, are polychronic, that is, people typically handle several activities at the same time. Educators may assume that their own familiarity with public policy is shared by parents of children with disabilities.

Schools must make a sincere commitment to consider parents as partners in their children's education. Professionals who are attempting to work and communicate with parents of children with disabilities should be prepared to support the parents' rights and responsibilities. In essence, professionals should adopt the role of advocate. Educators and other professionals should recognise parents' needs for the following:

i) Assurance that they should not feel guilty about their child's disability.
ii) Acceptance of their feelings without labelling.
iii) Acceptance of them as people, rather than as a category.
iv) Help in seeing the positive aspects of the future.
v) Recognition of what a big job it is to raise a child with disabilities and help in finding programmes, services, and financial resources to make it possible for them to do the job with dignity.

Using these guidelines for communication, teachers and other professionals can assist parents of culturally diverse children with disabilities not only to combat feelings of isolation, but also to achieve a sense of belonging.

Strategies of Language Teaching and Learning

Language is of prime importance in communication among individuals and between groups of people. Most individuals are born into and brought up in only one language. Communication between people with different language backgrounds is always to a greater or lesser extent problematic. In plurilingual societies and communities language(s) and language use planning is a first requirement. For example, such nations will have to sort out what language(s) to promote to the status of 'national' language, what language(s) to select for use in their educational systems as language(s) of instruction, and what (foreign) language(s) to offer to pupils to learn in school besides their native language.

In international plurilingual organisations members have to work out arrangements as to what language(s) to use for internal, institutional communication. Language is also fundamental in forming and expressing both individual and group identities. Human beings at a very young age become so much accustomed to the language of their surroundings that they lose the natural capacity to properly perceive the sound system of all other languages. They feel at one with their mother-tongue'; the language in question forms part of the individual's identity.

Similarly, people who share the same language tend to look upon that language as an essential element of their group identity. It is not unusual for conflicts between groups to centre around or culminate in a linguistic conflict. Not only is the learning of—and communicating in other—languages a hard job to achieve for most people, but the adoption itself of such languages also often meets with feelings of emotional resistance.

Therefore, there are languages and language use problems at a variety of levels and in a great variety of domains. Arrangements for all these levels and domains all, one way or another, require language political decisions. The internal language situation differs widely from nation to nation. Whether a country is classified as 'monolingual', 'bilingual' or 'plurilingual', greatly depends first of all on what one's definition of 'language' is. Language is a phenomenon that appears in many forms.

Only very few countries are truly monolingual; some countries pretend to be monolingual—usually by ignoring or underplaying the existence of minority languages, whether indigenous or brought in by immigrants. Most countries, therefore, are pluri- or multilingual. Multilingual countries display great variety in their choice of the language(s) of national intercourse. Often a choice is made for one language, occasionally for two or three. The language chosen is usually spoken by a majority of the population.

The criteria for selecting the national language(s) are diverse. Ideally, the choice "should result in the smallest possible disruption to the social structure". The main objective in choosing one or a very restricted number of national languages is usually the improvement of the internal communication process. A related, but often not articulated, objective is to build a more homogeneous nation, a nation that will feel united around its 'national' language, as a vital part of the nation's identity. Loyalty to a shared language may foster group identity.

The native language is often consciously used to help group formation and it is quite common for people to think that "one language, one nation" is a principle of essential importance in the creation and the preservation of the nation state. The 'national' language has, thus, become a major patriotic issue and a key symbol of nationalism, which phenomenon has been particularly characteristic of nation-building in Europe since the early nineteenth century. Whatever the motives, the choosing of a national language always implies reducing and simplifying linguistic variety.

The fact that language is an important factor in both individual and group identification, makes language, in general, a very sensitive subject. Language is embedded in culture; language utterances cannot be made outside the context of a certain culture nor be fully interpreted separately from this culture. And, also, culture requires expression in language; therefore, culture cannot truly thrive without a language in which it can be expressed. For most people, this bond between language and culture is so strong that language and culture are invariably mentioned in one breath and that their fates are regarded as inseparable.

A threat to linguistic variety is interpreted as a threat to cultural diversity. And, if cultural diversity is looked upon as a 'great wealth', as a treasure that should be cherished and guarded, the same is said of linguistic diversity. Any measure affecting the state and position of a language is, therefore, seen as a threat to the related culture. In international organisations like the European Union it is quite common to hear the view expressed that the existing multi-formity of both cultures and languages should at all times be maintained and, what is more, be promoted.

However, statements to that effect are not always devoid of rhetorical exaggeration. The close link that holds between language and culture also manifests itself, for the many different language (sub-)variants, in more or less corresponding culture (sub-)variants. Just as the national language is a variable and varying phenomenon, the national culture is much less of a monolithic entity than it is often made out to be. Moreover, however closely linked languages and cultures may be, the link between each specific pair is hardly ever altogether unique.

In general, every individual language has the capacity to express various cultures and, also, that every individual culture may be expressed in a number of different languages. The loss, therefore, of a particular language does not necessarily entail the concomitant loss of the related culture. And finally, the relations that languages have with cultures can vary considerably in strength, i.e., there are degrees to which the content of languages is culture-specific. For example, the culture-specific content of many technically specialised languages can be very limited, especially when the language in question is used worldwide by the occupational group concerned.

If all risk of ambiguity is to be precluded in international communication between people from different language and culture backgrounds, optimal transparency of the language used must be ensured. In international contexts the issues underlying the sensitivity that adheres to the subject of the national language, are equally prominent, if not more. If in a multilingual communicative setting only one language is used as the working-language, mother-tongue speakers of the preferred language have a natural advantage over those who are non-native to that language.

Skilful and smart use of language is, at all times, a powerful tool in negotiations, but the additional advantage that one derives from being able to rely on one's native language in communication with non-natives, is a real asset if one is seeking to exercise dominance over one's conversation partners. It is, therefore, quite understandable in itself that language groups or nations should want to promote their language at the cost of other languages.

The national or international supremacy of a language is the outcome of the particular language-group's or country's economic and political power. Whenever that kind of power is lacking, it cannot be created simply by gaining a prominent position for the country's language. In international organisations, especially if the members together bring in a great variety of languages, an important language political issue is what arrangement to choose for internal, institutional communication purposes.

In cooperative organisations such as the United Nations or the European Union, where all member-states are fundamentally equal, it is common to take the view that no one should be handicapped because of the status of his native language within that organisation. International organisations, because of this, sometimes opt for full equality of all the members' languages. European Union (EU), in which the present 15 member-states have a total of eleven working languages at their disposal, a few countries sharing the same language; for instance, Ireland and the United Kingdom have English in common and Austria and Germany German.

With such a large number of working-languages, however, effective mutual understanding can at times be very hard to achieve and the communication process can be very cumbersome and inefficient in terms of time and energy spent. It is practically impossible, of course, to provide for full translation and simultaneous interpretation facilities for eleven languages under all circumstances, i.e., in all official and informal settings where members get together for deliberations on matters of vital importance to them; just consider the organisational and logistic measures involved. But even if such facilities can be provided, their contribution to an optimal understanding and communication is less effective than is commonly expected.

The quality of translation, in particular of simultaneous interpretation, hardly ever reaches perfection and, unavoidably, is regularly deficient up to a point. The time lags that occur in simultaneous interpretation between the moment of utterance and the moment of hearing can be very annoying and, thus, may impede correct understanding. Communication may also be hampered by other causes. When within an organisation like the EU a general feeling arises that a diminution of the number of working-languages should be considered seriously, it turns out to be a difficult and complicated matter to solve what kind of arrangements to make in order to minimise to a more or less acceptable degree the handicaps of those members whose national languages are to be struck off the list and, at the same time, achieve the highest possible degree of both quality and effectiveness of communication.

The organisational setting constitutes its own 'domain of language use', the communicative needs of which are best served by using only a specific subset of the linguistic material available. The specialised language variants of such domains of language use, although primarily characterised by that kind of 'reduction', usually also exhibit their own specific features of jargon and style; the specific variant of 'institutional' language use is sometimes referred to as 'bureaucratese'. The higher the degree of specificity engendered by the particular domain of language use of an international institution, the more neutral with respect to 'cultural load' the language variant becomes.

Whereas communicating in any other but one's own native language may at all times be problematic, having to receive one's education in a non-native language is as a rule far worse. This is true for all school subjects, but it is especially true for initial literacy teaching. When instruction is supplied in the native language, the expansion of known concepts and the acquisition of new ones-achieved, from early childhood, in the native tongue- can proceed smoothly and naturally and is not hindered or complicated by the additional learning hurdle of having to acquire the matching linguistic tools in another language.

However, there are numerous reasons and circumstances which may make it desirable, necessary and/or inevitable to give all or part of the instruction in a non-native language. In fact, a great many youngsters receive all their instruction in (an)other language(s) than their mother-tongue, which is particularly true if we also include all those born into local and regional dialects. Languages may be so 'small', i.e., spoken by so few people, that no instructional materials have been produced in them and/or no teachers are available trained to give instruction through these languages.

Using the native language may also be considered undesirable and, therefore, the redressing of such adverse conditions inconvenient, if—for whatever reasons—the establishment of the favoured 'national' language has been proclaimed a major educational goal. The actual educational results of instruction through a non-native language are generally affected by the particular linguistic situation of the learner.

It does make a difference if the pupil's native language is also the language of the surrounding societal setting and not just that of his particular home situation. There are more such reasons for deliberately choosing a non-native language for instructional purposes, even if from an educational point of view there is no actual necessity for it. When a country lacks proper provisions for further and higher education, one may choose as the language of instruction the national language of the country that students preferably go to for continued studies.

These and similar situations have in common that the ultimate goal is to provide people with the best linguistic tool to get the best possible education; the pupils concerned, at least in the long run, wind up receiving all their instruction in the non-native language. Whenever there is a possibility of giving the instruction in the minority mother tongue, experience and tradition have it that the best practice is to start initial instruction off in the mother tongue, then to introduce the non-native language by its side, and later to have the non-native language gradually take over altogether.

The major focus in bilingual education is the learning of a minority language, mostly by the natives of the minority language concerned but also sometimes by majority language group students. Learning another language, when it is the language daily surrounding the learner, is a much more intensive and more 'natural' experience than learning another language when it is only 'available' in the 'unnatural' surroundings of the classroom situation.

The internal language situations of countries differ, but so do countries differ one from the other in their relations with neighbouring countries and with the international organisations in which they participate. The factors that have to be accounted for in the decision-making process, may be socio-economic, e.g., the amount of foreign trade with different parts of the world and countries. But they may also be psychological and educational.

Different countries may well attach different weights to such diverging needs as their commercial and cultural interests. Once a policy decision has been taken that a particular is to be learned and taught, the actual learning and teaching still has to be given shape. It is at the level of the classroom that the learning of concrete language material, in a way didactically most suited to the individual learners involved, has to take place.

Native or native-like competence is usually very hard to achieve, if at all. For most people—there are exceptions to the rule, of course—such accomplishment is just not possible and, if it is, only at the expense of a great deal of effort. Fortunately, for non-natives to be capable of communicating in the foreign language at an acceptable level that kind of full and maximum competence is not always a requirement. The kind and level of competence required, for one thing, greatly depends on the situation(s) in which the non-native will have to function.

The major concern in classrooms is to find ways to make the learners achieve the desired level of competence in the foreign language. There may be other objectives, such as instilling an understanding of the culture of the country and, as part of that, of the related literature, but the primary interest lies in the acquisition of a command of the language. But, also in the days that the learning of explicitly formulated rules of the new language formed part of the objective, rule-learning very often was not a goal in itself, but served the other didactic purpose of supporting and contributing to the acquisition of the command of the language in question. Now that rule-learning is not an end in itself anymore, when it occurs, it occurs as a didactic tool in the learning process. Its role as such is very much a moot point, which it probably always has been except in the days of the traditional grammar-translation method, when the teaching of (modern) languages was very much modelled on the teaching of the classical languages.

The tool of making learners learn—usually by heart—explicitly formulated rules of the foreign language has come under serious criticism from many, because, it is said, for high-level command of both first and second languages 'knowledge' of rules is only required in the sense of a full and fully automatised control of the underlying rule-system, and, moreover, mastery of rules in first language competence comes about in a very 'natural' way, it seems, without any interference on the basis of explicitly formulated rules. However, in general it is a didactic misconception to think that the specific characteristics of the objective, in this case of language competence, should either be represented in or fully prescribe the teaching content and that nothing else should.

In classrooms there are three major categories of variables at work that each individually and in interaction with each other determine what is the optimal didactic arrangement for each specific situation. The variables cluster around the learner, the teacher and the subject matter, i.e., the language competence in question. There is no classroom setting like any other classroom setting, which means that there is a great deal of variation in what one calls 'best practice'. Learners of different ages are differently motivated, they approach their learning tasks differently, they bring with them different learning careers, i.e., they may have developed different approaches to and preferences for tackling learning problems.

Bilingual Education programmes

Bilingual education is the use of two languages. Bilingual education historically emerged as an answer to address profound educational, cultural, and political injustices, and has never been exclusively a linguistic issue. Bilingualism has become a primary concern in public education and learning, especially in contexts with multiple cultural groups.

In Europe in particular, the principal linguistic shift since the second half of the eighteenth century was related to an increasing sense of national identity and thus a process of language homogenisation. While the Ottoman and Austrian empires were declining, new players in the European geopolitical scene emerged. Even if old empires used official languages (*lingua franca*), the State did not have a systematic policy of language assimilation.

Religious languages, such as Hebrew, Arabic, or Latin, have maintained a special status. These empires were indeed multinational and multilingual, while the new European powers were based on both a strong national identity and a policy of linguistic homogenisation. Countries including Germany, Italy, France, and England became increasingly national-centred entities as well as colonial powers. One's nationality came to be defined by a language. Language was identified as the main criterion in defining nationality and citizenship.

The situation in the United States is typical of many other situations. Since the early 1960s, the issue of bilingualism has been linked to the debate on cultural diversity, immigration policy, and the democratisation of our society. Over time, an awareness of the interdependence of civil rights, women's rights, environmental concerns, and peace issues converged to introduce bilingual education into the political arena. In addition, the number of minority language children rapidly grew as a result of both economic and political immigration. Using the Civil Rights Act as a platform, minority groups, particularly Latinos and Native Americans, pushed for the use of their native language in public schools as a method of allowing their children equal opportunity to public education. This movement was extremely strong in Texas, where Chicano students and parents protested against the discriminatory policies practiced by the Anglo school staff and administration. Leaders within the movement sought to decolonise those institutions that contributed to the continuation of subordination and exploitation of the Chicanos by Anglo-Americans.

During the 1990s, Maori activists in New Zealand also experimented with a similar process to that of the Chicano people in the United States. They withdrew their children from the Anglo education system and worked toward establishing a separate Maori education system. Many Maori people argued that Maori rights to cultural autonomy, as well as to political sovereignty and economic self-sufficiency, were guaranteed by the treaty that was signed by Maori leaders and the colonial army during the nineteenth century. Many Maori people have succeeded in establishing their own educational institutions. These are seen as a means of resuscitating the Maori language, of protecting cultural autonomy, and of developing curricula that teach tribal knowledge and approach the academic disciplines from Maori perspectives.

In Latin America, the decolonisation process for indigenous people has been centred on three issues: preservation of ancestral territories, amelioration of economic conditions, and local control over educational institutions. In Peru, indigenous organisations have played a key role in implementing bilingual intercultural programmes as an alternative to the hegemonic model of schooling promoted by the evangelic North-American missionaries with the complicity of the Peruvian state.

In Europe, linguistic diversity branched into two different directions. On the one hand, central governments allowed minimal inclusion of regional indigenous languages in the educational system and in the areas of regional, cultural, and artistic expression. On the other hand, both host and native countries of immigrants agreed to increase the use of native languages in extracurricular activities intended for second generation immigrants. In others words, Europe did not treat local and "imported" linguistic diversity similarly.

While legislation on bilingual public education for European regional minorities was progressively implemented, there was no significant public funding available to immigrant students, particularly those who came from Africa and Asia. In addition, the continual economic dependency on western countries has contributed to cultural dependency that included an overvaluation of European languages.

School culture is not neutral but rather a particular culture that serves the interest of those who occupy dominant positions in the society. Determining the distinguishing characteristics of bilingual education programmes is an effective way to understand their dynamics and to identify the varying rationale among each programme. There are six models of managing linguistic diversity in formal education:

i) segregated language remediation,

ii) transitional bilingual education,

iii) language developmental bilingual education,

iv) integrated-enrichment bilingual education,

v) two-way bilingual education, and

vi) neo-colonial bilingual education..

Segregated language remediation: This model is not commonly considered as a bilingual education programme, it is the most commonly used method in addressing language diversity in schools and therefore warrants discussion. The goal of segregated language remediation is to rapidly mainstream children into the dominant language. Typically, children identified as having "limited English proficiency" (LEP) are separated from regular classrooms and spend a variable amount of time with specialists who teach the dominant language.

In Switzerland, "accommodation classrooms" are organised to quickly equip minority language students with dominant language skills that allow their integration in the mainstream classrooms. This experience facilitates the integration of students into their grade-age class regardless of their previous school experiences. It is also an opportunity for students to share their life and language experiences with students in the same or similar situations from all over the world.

Unfortunately, the lack of teacher proficiency in languages other than the national language, and the pressure to successfully integrate immigrant children within the regular classroom, convert the "accommodation classrooms" from a potential medium of integration to a powerful instrument of monolingual mainstreaming.

Transitional bilingual education: Transitional bilingual education is also known as early-exit bilingual education, a model whose primary goal is to "mainstream" students to all dominant-language classrooms. This model uses native-language instruction to help students initially keep up in other subjects, but it eventually shifts to dominant-language instruction. Thus, the native language possesses only transitional or temporary value. In the end, proficiency in the dominant language is that which is the most important.

Language developmental bilingual education: Developmental bilingual education, also known as language maintenance bilingual education, strives to achieve fluent bilingualism and biliteracy as well as academic excellence. It typically phases in the dominant language through a more gradual manner than transitional bilingual programmes and continues to develop students' skills in the native language after they have become fully proficient in the dominant language.

A little known version of this model can be found in immigrant-children education in many European countries. Typically, the immigrants' country of origin organises classes in the native language in schools or community centres. These courses, also known as language and cultural heritage courses, emphasise the cultural heritage of the parents' country and have minimal pedagogical links with the host country school system.

Integrated-enrichment bilingual education: Integrated-enrichment programmes, first introduced in Canada, were developed from the concept of immersion. There are differentiate two types of integrated-enrichment programmes: foreign-language immersion and native-language immersion.

Foreign language immersion is a model in which language-majority students are instructed primarily or exclusively through sheltered instruction in a second language, later combined with native language classes. This model follows an additive approach, the overriding goal being functional bilingualism with no cost to academic achievement. French language immersion in Canada is a typical example of this model.

The instrumental value of "foreign language" as an economic tool is a central key in the success of these programmes. There are various possibilities of using communication and a content-based approach to teach second languages, with little or no use of students' first language.

Native language immersion is a model in which indigenous minority students are taught in an endangered minority language through sheltered instruction. This model promotes revitalisation of a community's vernacular and strengthens students' cultural identity while at the same time fostering academic achievement.

"Neo-colonial" bilingual education is not very well documented in the pedagogical literature. This model can be found in former European colonies that existed in Africa and Asia. After achieving their independence, many of these countries continued to use English, French, or Portuguese as the language medium of instruction. This maintenance of the colonial legacy can be explained by political, economic, and historical factors.

When minority language students are emerged in an adequate bilingual learning environment, they reap the continual benefits of being able to communicate in more than one language or dialect. Supporters of bilingual education consider that children cannot learn in a language they do not understand. The most important relationship between language and culture that gets to the heart of what is lost when you lose a language is that most of the culture is in the language and is expressed in the language.

Most of the bilingual education programmes tended to focus more on disabling than empowering minority students. Indeed, empowerment must include, in addition to the school sphere, communities, neighbourhoods, and families. In general approach to bilingual education posits the necessity of stronger links between the use of language in school and other contexts. While the mainstream classroom is based on a "transmission-banking" model, with the main goal of domestication and perpetuation of the social *status quo*, an effective bilingual education programme should challenge this model and drive the classroom pedagogy toward a liberatory, more "reciprocal-interactive pedagogy".

A fundamental principal of bilingual multicultural education is that the student's language and culture will be accepted and fully incorporated into the classroom climate in order for a meaningful pedagogical experience to occur. The feelings, attitudes, values, self-concepts concerns, and appreciations of all students are essential elements for the entire educational process to be fully experienced and need critical consideration. Often the affective environment, the interactions between students and students, and between students and teachers, i.e., the classroom climate, is overlooked as being important to the student's social and emotional development and educational efficacy.

But for those who have truly experienced this universal human activity, there is always an expectation of a joyful subjective feeling that is recognised as ever potential by both teacher and learner in every pedagogical situation. The learner has felt and seeks again the good feeling of the mastery and understanding of a skill, or the consummatory experience of insight, appreciation, and understanding of ideas, or the thrill of discovering something not known before, or the feeling of accomplishment that comes with making sense of the world.

The teacher also has experienced and seeks again the joy or success found in the purposeful pedagogical activity, the empathetic sharing of the joy of the learner, and the basic human satisfaction of freely giving to another human being those things that nurture their growth as individuals and as social beings. The subjective experience is an important part of the process.

The bilingual multicultural classroom climate has physical and social, as well as intellectual forces and conditions that impinge upon a student. Also, the climate acting with other forces in and out of a classroom offers the student the psychological experiences of exploration, limitation, and self-impact. In turn, the social relations, among the students as a group and between the students and the teacher will significantly influence the cognitive and affective learning outcomes. That successful affective and cognitive experiences within a classroom will guarantee an increase in positive attitudes toward school. Nevertheless, the unsuccessful affective and cognitive experiences within a classroom will guarantee an increase in negative attitudes toward school-related activities.

Limitations

There are limitations of bilingual education programmes within the formal educational system. Schools are not producing significant "sociocultural productivity". The knowledge that students receive in school is rarely related or transferable to other settings outside of school. One possible solution to this crisis is to shift the focus from exclusively within the school to other domains.

Historically, most forms of schooling have been conceptually constructed as mechanisms of repression, as a way to screen, discipline, and regulate the instruction of others. Social justice has never been a point of discussion in formal schooling. Formal schooling has little power on social injustice. Each society fashions the school system to serve the interests of dominant groups. In order to reverse the traditional thinking about bilingual education, it is necessary to rid it of the exclusive focus on school settings.

The socio-historical theory provides a good tenet for understanding the interdependence of the individual and society and how each creates and is created by each other. As a cultural tool, bilingualism plays a central position in promoting critical literacy among the "oppressed". Indeed, even though contextualised language presents a step against domestication, we still need to go one step further and question the power relationships within the global society.

Bilingual education is not only a linguistic debate; it inherently implies a position of colonialism and cultural pluralism. Critical pedagogy provides a possibility to go beyond this. In contrast to many contemporary pedagogical frameworks that ignore the persistence of imperialism in international and national relations, critical pedagogy addresses more than just the learning process and denounces the structural inequality between countries and between different social and cultural groups in each country:

Both critical pedagogy and multicultural education need to address themselves to the adaptive persistence of capitalism and to issues of capitalist imperialism and its specific manifestations of accumulative capacities through conquest. In other words, critical pedagogy needs to establish a project of emancipation centered on the transformation of property relations and the creation of a just system of appropriation and distribution of social wealth.

References

Baca, L. M., Cervantes, H. T., *The bilingual special education interface*, Columbus, OH: Merill, 1989.

Bernard (ed.), *Concise Encyclopedia of Educational Linguistics*, London, Pergamon, 1999.

Baker, Colin, Sylvia Prys Jones, *Encyclopedia of Bilingualism and Bilingual Education*, Clevedon (Multilingual Matters), 1998

Byram, Michael (ed.), *Encyclopedia of Language Teaching and Learning*, London/New York, Routledge, 2000.

Carrasquillo, A., “Bilingual special education: The important connection”, In A. Carrasquillo and R. Baecher (eds.), *Teaching the bilingual special education students,* NY: Ablex, 1990.

Carrasquillo, A. and Rodriguez, V., *Language minority students in the mainstream classroom*, England: Multilingual. Council for Exceptional Children, 1993.

Cummins, J., *Bilingualism and special education: Issues in assessment and pedagogy*, San Diego, CA: College-Hill, 1984.

Cummins, Jim, David Corson (eds.), *Bilingual Education*, 1997.

“Empowering minority students: A framework for intervention”, *Harvard Educational Review,* 56 (1), 18-36, 1986.

Hamayan, E. V., Kwiat, J. A., and Perlman, R., *Assessment of language minority students: A handbook for educators*, Chicago: Illinois Resource Centre, 1985.

Martin Puetz (ed.), *Language Choices. Conditions, constraints, and consequences*, Amsterdam/Philadelphia, John Benjamins Publishing Company, 1997.

Ramirez, J.D., & Douglas, D., *Language minority parents and the school: Bridging the gap*, Sacramento: California State Dept. of Education, Office of Bilingual Bicultural Education.

Trueba, H. T., "*Success or failure? Learning and the language minority students*", Rowley, MA: Newbury, 1987.

Wodak, Ruth, David Corson (eds.), *Language Policy and Political Issues in Education*, 1997.

Wittrock, M. C., "Constructing useful theories of teaching English from recent research in the cognitive process of language", In J. Squire (ed.), *The dynamics of language*, Urbana, Ill: Clearinghouse in Reading and Communication Skills, 1987.

6

Online Technologies in Multicultural Education

The possibilities that this current era offers for multiculturalism and multicultural education seem endless. In addition to adding new areas such as disability studies and queer studies, cultural studies, post-colonial, post-modern, and post-structuralist studies all attempt to push past conventional and essentialised thinking about race, class, and gender. But these "new studies" are not unproblematic. Multicultural education's seeming allegiance to the triumvirate of race, class, and gender may have rendered it less useful to scholars and practitioners who have to work with the complexities of identities that do not fit into fixed categories.

Multiculturalism and multicultural education have access to more expanded methodologies such as narrative inquiry, counter stories, historical ethnographies, autobiography, portraiture, and a full range of indigenous projects: claiming, testimonies, celebrating survival, remembering, indigenising, intervening, revitalising, gendering, connecting, envisioning, reframing, restoring, returning, democratising, naming, protecting, creating, and sharing.

The present trend in multiculturalism and multicultural education is globalisation. Communication satellites, fibre optic cables, the internet, and e mail bring every corner of the world into our homes. Almost everywhere in the world, people have access to CNN, ESPN, etc. The enduring question facing multicultural education is what to do as a school reform effort in the face of this rapid social and cultural change. Multicultural education faces pressure from forces of school reform and standardisation on one end of the spectrum and the complexities and changes occasioned by globalisation on the other.

ROLE OF TECHNOLOGIES

At its most fundamental level, multicultural education represents an orientation to schooling and the teaching-learning process that is grounded in the democratic ideals of justice and equality. According to James A. Banks, a leading scholar in the field of multicultural education, there are five critical dimensions of multicultural education: content integration, knowledge construction, prejudice reduction, equity pedagogy, and empowering school culture and social structure. The role of technology in these critical dimenions of multicultural education is breifly described in this section.

Technology in Content Integration

The goal of content integration is to expand the curriculum by incorporating contributions of diverse cultures into traditional disciplines of study. Arguably, this dimension is easily realised through technology. For instance, teachers at all levels have used the world wide web to extend the available learning resources. Electronic mail and multimedia technologies promote communication and interactions between diverse groups with the purpose of helping students learn more about content they study in subject areas as social studies, science, psychology, and even foreign language.

Educators who acknowledge potential benefits of a merger between technology and multicultural education call for updating the physical infrastructures of schools. In schools where such updates have occurred, teachers are making widespread use of the internet and other computer-based technology. And the knowledge and skills students acquire in these schools typically are being reinforced by computer availability and internet access in their homes.

This reality contrasts sharply with that of students from poor/working class backgrounds who attend schools where the notion of re-wiring for internet access may seem superfluous in light of the absence of basic resources. Nor are these students likely to have internet access at home.

Citing a 1999 report of the US National Telecommunications and Information Administration, Gorski reports that "African American and Latino households are only about one-third as likely to have access to the internet from home as Asian, Asian American, and Pacific Islander households. The same group is only two-fifths as likely to have access as White households". This situation is reflective of the "digital divide" phenomenon. Thus, while technology can facilitate the content integration in the teaching-learning process, educators must be aware that in some circumstances this dimension of multicultural education will need to be addressed by other means due to lack of access to technology.

Technology in Knowledge Construction

Knowledge construction builds upon content integration by making explicit the worldviews and perspectives that inform knowledge claims. Similarly, it expands the legitimate sources of knowledge by helping learners recognise that their own experiences both within and beyond school are viable foundations for acquiring knowledge and skills. Teacher educators are being called upon to use technology to promote and reinforce the knowledge construction process.

Part of acquiring facility in knowledge construction is understanding phenomenon from the perspectives of others. To this end, teacher educators are making use of internet technology to promote more critical engagement with subject matter. For example, Merryfield discusses advantages of threaded discussions in an online graduate course. Student-generated threads facilitate a class learning community that allows those of diverse cultural and national origins to perspective-take while simultaneously examining their own ideas about cultural diversity.

Technology to Reduce Prejudice

Prejudice reduction is about eliminating all forms of bigotry. Also, it involves promoting healthy personal identity devoid of the tendency or need to denigrate those who differ from self. Multimedia presentations and distance learning technologies are being used to establish learning exchanges between students of diverse cultural backgrounds and thereby reduce prejudice and stereotyping.

Likewise, technology is being used to promote positive self-concept and foster positive relationships between students from diverse backgrounds in geographically diverse areas. Such efforts have included videoconferences, computer conferences, interactions on the web, and e-pals. Technologies used with middle grade students have included interactive compressed video and use of two-way televised communication systems via telephone lines. Teacher education students are using distance learning technology, multimedia, and e mail to engage in cross-cultural and diverse regional interactions with other prospective teachers.

Technolgy for Equity Pedagogy

Writers interested in the nascent relationship between technology and multicultural education are discussing the urgency of using technology to address the various ways in which learners from diverse backgrounds best acquire school knowledge and skills. Nevertheless, it is difficult to discern whether current efforts to merge technology and multicultural education are addressing this fourth dimension directly. Indeed, some writers are concerned that technology may inadvertently privilege certain ways of processing information while it devalues others.

An important issue for many contemporary educators, particularly in the university setting, is whether internet technology is in any way superior to face-to-face instruction. It would appear that one advantage internet technology holds over face-to-face classroom format is in its ability to provide educators and students wide access to a cross-cultural professional and learning community. This can be accommodated through e-mail, bulletin boards, and chatroom sites.

Technology for Empowering Culture

In order to provide high quality experiences for all students, many traditional aspects of schools will need to be reconfigured. This is referred to as empowering school culture and social structures. Its ultimate purpose is to change the taken-for-granted policies and practices of schools that, while useful to some students, have greatly diminished the schooling experience for many others. For example, Arias describes how the new California State University, Monterey Bay, is making extensive use of technology to provide access to higher education to the burgeoning population of Latinos and other people of colour who historically have been excluded from such opportunities. Throughout the US, access to university courses and degree programmes are being made available to students by expanded distance education opportunities that now routinely include courses offered online in part or in their entirety.

Creating a Learning Revolution

Digital technologies are now providing an historic opportunity for fundamental and global-scale changes in children's learning and education. They are making possible a "learning revolution" in education. We believe that these new digital technologies can transform not only how children learn, but also what children learn, and who they learn with.

— *How children learn.* Digital technologies can enable children to become more active and independent learners, taking charge of their own learning through direct exploration, expression, and experience. The focus shifts from "being taught" to "learning".

— *What children learn.* Much of what children learn in schools today was designed for the era of paper-and-pencil. With new digital technologies, children can undertake projects (and learn concepts) that were seen as too complex for children in the pre-digital era.

— *Who children learn with.* Global connectedness can enable new "knowledge-building communities" in which children (and adults) around the globe collaborate on projects and learn from one another. These efforts require new multicultural, multilingual, and multimodal approaches to learning.

Although declining costs will make digital technologies increasingly available to children around the world, access to computers and internet connections is not enough. Many of the software products that are being developed for children today serve to narrow, rather than broaden, children's intellectual horizons. To create a true learning revolution, we must create technologies that support a new vision of learning and a new vision of children. The following principles will guide us to achieve this goal:

— *Direct exploration.* The traditional view is that children learn about the world directly until preschool, but then they need to be "taught" more advanced ideas. Our goal is to develop digital technologies that enable children to continue to learn ever more advanced ideas by direct exploration and experimentation. For example, children who live in remote villages should be able to contribute directly to their community's agricultural efforts by using computers connected globally to the internet, and locally to sensors, to run experiments on the quality of soil, air, and vegetation.

— *Direct expression.* New media will enable children to relate their own stories and ideas — and relate them to a much broader and more diverse audience — rather than having adults do the talking for them. The traditional view is that children should focus on "absorbing" ideas from adults, not on expressing their own ideas. Even what children know about themselves and their culture is what they hear from adults. Our goal is to go beyond this traditional view and develop digital technologies that enable children to express themselves to others through storytelling, communicating, designing, and inventing in new ways—in effect, to find their own voice.

— *Direct experience.* In the future, children will no longer rely only on their parents for reports of the great big world out there. Instead, they will experience it directly through their own personal contacts with other people around the globe. Through electronic eyes and ears, they will be able to see how the other side of the world looks and sounds. This experience will diminish the impact of national frontiers, although local cultures — what children experience in their own schoolyards and homes — will remain important. Perhaps most important, children will develop a different sense of themselves as intellectual agents — as valuable members of real and virtual communities. Children will become accustomed to expressing themselves across boundaries of geography, culture, language, and age.

— *Multicultural.* Most technologies support only a limited set of cultural styles and approaches. With global connectedness comes both a need and an opportunity for more encompassing approaches, encouraging participation by children from all different cultures. Our goal is to develop new digital technologies that provide multiple paths of entry and multiple patterns of use, while also encouraging children around the world to share and learn about one another's cultural traditions.

— *Multilingual.* To date, the great variety of languages spoken around the world has been perceived as a major obstacle to the development of a global community. With global connectedness comes an ever greater need for children to "speak a common language", and an ever greater opportunity for children to learn more about one another's languages — and about language in general. Our goal is to develop new tools that enable children to communicate with one another across linguistic boundaries, while supporting their learning of other languages, and enhancing the value of their own.

— *Multimodal.* The channels of communication between children and computers have been extremely limited: keystrokes and mouse clicks in one direction, text and graphics in the other. By enabling computers to understand and produce gestures and other forms of nonverbal communication, we will enrich the nature of the interaction between children and computers. By the same token, computers that understand verbal and non-verbal communication can open up computing to a broader range of ages and cultural traditions.

Web-oriented Multicultural Education

The world wide web (WWW) transcends the traditional practices of connecting people with information to connect people with other people. It facilitates an atmosphere in which voices, stories, reflections and interactions reach beyond those available in the classroom, school, or community. It facilitates each of the strands essential to multicultural reconstructionist education such as critical pedagogy, interaction, and inclusion through various interactive and hyper-navigable technologies. Web designers employ critical pedagogy through technologies such as "WWW Board" which allow students to read and reflect on a passage or story on line, and to read and reflect on other students' reflections. While students were previously capable of doing this within their classroom, web designers facilitate an experience in which students can share with other people—other cultures—from around the world.

Web designers address the interaction strand of multicultural education by offering interactive forums and by making themselves available for interaction. Forums include "chat rooms" in which people can interact in real time and discussion boards on which people can post a question, comment, or response and through which others can read those posts and respond. Web designers can also provide links to their e-mail addresses or "Guestbook" forums to allow visitors to communicate with them directly.

The web facilitates inclusion through interactive technologies as well as hyper-navigation. Most websites include a list of links to other sites of similar interest. These links allow the user to move (or hyper-navigate) from one site to another—possibly from one continent to another—with a click of the mouse. The designer of a website about Custer might offer a link to a Native-American's site on Custer. While a book might contain a list of sources or a citation to link readers to another source, the web can offer the resource, and a direct line to it, at the click of a button.

Unfortunately, the multicultural potential of the web remains unrealised and unemployed by educators and education website designers. What the web can facilitate and what designers can offer is not reflected in the majority of educational websites currently online. Most educational websites facilitate little interaction above an e mail link to the designer. Content is usually presented in a fashion that does not give students the opportunity to reflect, interact, or challenge the information. Designers usually offer links to sites with similar perspectives instead of those with different perspectives. Even sites that purport to be "multicultural" often offer a very uni-cultural selection of links.

Strategies for Online Networking

The internet offers many different approaches for networking and interacting with people. Some strategies for networking and interacting online are:

E mail webmasters: Most websites have a link to the maintainer's email address. Remember, the best multicultural resources are people. When you find a site that sparks your interest, send an e-mail to the designer or maintainer of the site describing your interest. If you have a question, comment, or challenge to a site's designer, don't be afraid to send it. The most they can do is not answer. If they do answer, the result may be a useful exchange and a learning experience for you both.

Online forums: Some websites house discussion forums such as WWWBoard or Hypernews. These forums allow you to post a message on a website which other visitors can then read and respond to. If you're looking for resources, have a question, or want to start a discussion strand, post a message. Also take the time to respond to others' questions if you can be of some assistance.

Join email discussion forums: Thousands of e mail-based discussion groups allow you to interact with large groups of other folks by distributing messages to each member of the group. If you have a specific interest area, you can surely find a number of groups related to that interest.

Multicultural Approach for Evaluating Educational WebSites

The criteria used to assess and evaluate traditional educational media such as accuracy of the information, critical analysis of possible bias, credibility of the author and/or publishing source, appropriateness and accessibility to the specified audience, timeliness, relevance to a particular subject area, validity of content, and effectiveness of aesthetic aspects can be directly applied to websites as well. Together with these traditional criteria, several new criteria must be incorporated into current models to holistically evaluate products of websites.

Unlike traditional educational media such as films, textbooks, and journals — all of which are usually subject to a rigorous review process before being made widely available to teachers and students — virtually anybody with access to a web server can create an educational web site. Generally, no entity comparable to a publishing company exists to help ensure the credibility or expertise of educational web designers or authors. Likewise, no formal review board examines the validity of the information on most educational web sites.

In the web, the line between commercial and informational distinctions so blatantly blurry. It is often difficult to ascertain whether a particular site is a purely commercial venture or a purely educational venture. In fact, it may be the case that no site fits the latter extreme. Since many websites are produced by unfamiliar sources, the users, must look deeper to uncover the bias of online educational products. Unlike the content of books or films, the information on web sites is not static. Used responsibly, this can be a strength of websites. Information can be updated any time, new information can be added, and old information can be removed.

With these challenges, it is imperative that new approaches for evaluating educational websites emerge focus special attention on the characteristics that differentiate the medium from other educational media.

The two related factors which highlight the need for a multicultural approach for evaluating educational websites.

First, despite the troubling number of educators who continue to equate it with Black History Month or an annual diversity festival, we must continue to push toward an actualisation of multicultural education that examines, critiques, and transforms all aspects of education. A tight focus only on curriculum or teaching styles or any one aspect of education does not constitute multicultural education. Multicultural education views the school as a social system that consists of highly interrelated parts and variables. Therefore, in order to transform the school to bring about educational equality, all the major components of the school must be substantially changed. A focus on any one variable in the school, such as the formalised curriculum, will not implement multicultural education. A second factor relates to the clear intersections between internet media and multicultural teaching and learning practices. The web transcends virtually all other educational media in its capacity for facilitating intercultural, interactive and collaborative teaching and learning.

A short consideration of current approaches for evaluating educational websites will provide points of critique and consideration for the development a new approach.

For the past several years, university librarians, educational and instructional technologists, and web developers have created checklists, outlines, and other schema for evaluating web resources. The range and variation of these models highlight the challenge of creating effective tools for evaluating a phenomenon and medium still in a state of infancy.

Some models, such as Bruce Leland's *Evaluating Web Sites: A Guide for Writers*, Joe Landsberger's *Evaluating Website Content*, and Elizabeth E. Kirk's *Evaluating Information Found on the Internet* rely solely on criteria developed for evaluating print resources. Though each of them, in introductions to their models, acknowledges the features differentiating the web from other media, all three fail to include evaluation criteria that focus on these features. Their criteria include authority, currency, bias, accuracy and credibility.

Other existing models for evaluating educational websites place emphasis on the unique characteristics, opportunities, and challenges of the medium. Esther Grassian's *Thinking Critically about World Wide Web Resources* attempts to narrow the proverbial chasm between education theory and instructional technology by including several items dealing with the effectiveness of a site's educational and graphical design. The staff of McIntyre Library at the University of Wisconsin-Eau Claire add a new dimension to the assessment process by including a "Comparability" criterion that asks whether comparable resources can be found in more traditional media, and whether those are more valuable and practical for the intended use. Their Ten C's for Evaluating Internet Sources also assesses the extent to which information on a site is updated, an important item for non-static web media.

Schrock's *Teaching Media Literacy in the Age of the Internet* contains a list of 26 evaluation criteria for teachers. Many focus on distinct characteristics of the internet, including:

— *Dates*: Does the site include a notation about when information was placed online or updated?
— *Efficiency*: How quickly does the page load on the screen?
— *Links*: Does the site contain original resources, or just links to other original resources? Are links appropriate?
— *Navigability*: Is the site's organisation obvious?
— *Quantity of information*: Is the site interactive, and will it be necessary to return to the site periodically for updated information?
— *Requirements*: Does the site insist on requirements (such as plug-in software) or registration?
— *Uniqueness*: Are the unique qualities of the web a strength (interactivity) or a weakness (blurred distinction between the educational and the commercial) of the site?

These models, by acknowledging and addressing the characteristics that differentiate the web from other educational media, represent a significant step in the improvement of educational website evaluation.

Grassian and Schrock journey a step further, each introducing at least one criterion that starts to examine important multicultural principles as actualised (or not actualised) in educational sites. Both include an item on accessibility for differently-abled users (e.g., text-only versions, large fonts, etc.). Schrock and the McIntyre Library staff at UW-Eau Claire mention the importance of applying critical thinking skills, both for evaluating sites and for preparing students to process information they find on sites.

The existing models and approaches fail to assess the extent to which educational websites utilise the multicultural potentialities of the internet medium. Furthermore, they fail to address nearly all multicultural teaching and learning principles: attention to varied learning styles, engagement and inclusion of diverse and divergent perspectives, active and participatory teaching and learning, etc. An approach grounded in these and other principles of multicultural education must both reconsider general educational product evaluation criteria and incorporate new criteria that examine the multicultural-educational worth of individual websites.

Through an understanding of educational evaluation, multicultural education, and the web as an educational medium, a list of seven criteria categories to help guide a multicultural approach for evaluating educational websites:

i) *Relevance and appropriateness.* Too often, a tendency exists in the field of educational technology to use new technology for the sake of using new technology, without a particular need or sense for how it will improve curricula or pedagogy. So while this category may appear to be an obvious first step in assessing a website or any educational product, it is also an important step in determining the contextual strength(s) or weakness(es) of a particular medium. It explores the extent to which the medium, content and target audience of a site are relevant and appropriate to your needs and target audience.

ii) *Credibility.* One cannot assume credibility or expertise in regards to a website as readily as they might with a textbook (although similar questions should be asked about textbook writers). We must be conscious of credibility both in terms of the author's authority and the trustworthiness of a site's content.

iii) *Bias Identification.* The focus should not only be on what information is included on a site — we must remember to consider what is not included, and the related implications. This criteria category critically examines the inclusiveness and exclusiveness of a site.

iv) *Accuracy.* The foundation of a multicultural curriculum is accuracy and completeness. This category addresses both of these intertwined concepts.

v) *Accessibility.* The internet was originally designed to provide people access to each other and information. If a resource is inaccessible because of coding problems or incompatibility with certain browsers or special-needs users, it fails to meet even the minimum requirements for an effective educational tool. And if a site author or sponsor is inaccessible through the site, he fails to take advantage of the fundamental nature of the inherently interactive internet technology. This category also reminds us that the supposed "global classroom" is globally exclusive of those who cannot afford to participate or who do not have access for some other reason — an important, but often forgotten point of dialogue related to the internet.

vi) *Navigability*. If your students cannot find their way around a site, it will not take long for collective disengagement to ensue.

vii) *Multiculturality*. The web has the capability to house educational opportunities consistent with the principles of multicultural teaching and learning to a greater extent than any other medium. Educational sites should reflect this capability.

Challenges

New technologies are dramatically altering every aspect of life from work to education. While television has been regularly denounced by educators for the "dumbing down" of youth, new multimedia technologies like CD-ROMs and internet websites produce new resources and material for expanding multicultural education.

Many current criticisms of the role of computer and multimedia technology in the school stem from an inability to grasp the nature and importance of computer literacy and to understand how new technologies can help revitalise multicultural education. This failure to embrace new technologies as a teaching device has been preceded by an uneven and never adequate use of film and television material in the classroom.

So-called "media" material was often used as a supplement, or as an excuse for the teacher to take a break from the arduous activity of interacting creatively with students—and is still used in this way. Yet rarely has media literacy been taught, and imaginative use of media materials in the classroom remains all-to-seldom—although creative use of computer and new multimedia material highlights how older media like photographic images, video documentary, and film can also immensely enhance instruction.

Within classrooms, as well as higher echelons of learning, media, computer, and technological literacies are rarely discussed. However, it is to be hoped that this situation may soon change under the pressures of the computerisation of multicultural education now underway. It appears as if a form of elitist blindness has emanated from far too many of the leading educational theorists and so-called experts regarding the significance and importance of recognising the enormous role of media in the everyday lives of both teacher and student. There is also a pervasive failure to employ these common and shared materials and media in a manner that intensifies and enhances the experience of multicultural education through teaching about the semiotic codes and ideological frames that organise and structure so much of media culture.

There is a general failure in developing critical skills and analytic abilities that empower both teacher and student, providing them with the skills to analytically criticise and interpret media culture. Moreover, critical media literacy in the computer era is necessary for understanding and navigating within ever more complex technological/ideological forms that require computer and multimedia literacy so as to enable students to utilise computers, CD-ROMs, the world wide web, and the internet.

Media and computer literacy will enable students to more actively seek information and knowledge, and also provides the skills to actually produce and develop their own cultural artifacts within both an educational setting and within a much wider pedagogical, philosophical, and practical context. It is indeed inspiring to see websites and other artifacts that students have already produced with computer and multimedia technologies, often collaboratively. In view of the increased role of computers in business, higher education, and everyday life, such skills will be necessary for full and creative participation in the societies of the rapidly approaching future.

It is therefore unfortunate that many influential educators and pedagogues have underemphasised and discredited the significance of media and computer literacies and productions, in lieu of outdated arguments which privilege the written word over other forms of cultural expression. It may be that this is the bias of the university professor, immersed in the publish or perish domain of the university, and is translated into hostility toward alternative multimedia pedagogies. The prejudice against computers and interactive multimedia may reflect technological incompetencies and phobia on the part of teachers who themselves have not mastered these technologies and cultural forms.

In a world of information overload, it is increasingly important to teach the skills of critical reading and analysis, and clear and concise writing. Moreover, a good classroom teacher can provide context, appropriate application of course material to the situation of the students, and a forum for discussion and live interaction that computers cannot provide. It is the responsibility of educators to make use of the most advanced technologies for multicultural educational purposes.

Teaching tools cannot fully replace teachers. The relationship between print media and multimedia technology, as well as between classroom teaching and computerised teaching tools, is not a choice of either/or, but is one of both/and. In this conception, multimedia is used to supplement print material and computers are deployed to supplement classroom teaching exercises. Yet rather than deploying new multimedia technologies, traditional educators persist in blaming media and technology for declining test scores and an alleged dumbing-down of youth — not unlike blaming the victim. These educators often propose or defend problematic tools like "V-Chips" in televisions to censor so-called sexually explicit or violent programming rather than teaching students to critically analyse and dissect representations of violence or other objectionable media material. Likewise, it is now fashionable to defend programs that will block home or school computers from objectionable content as the solution to allegedly debased and dangerous forms of computer culture.

The incorporation of media literacy programs within the public and university systems hardly requires anything more than a television set, VCR monitor, pretaped programs, and a teacher and/or professor who is trained, committed, and knowledgeable in basic critical media literacy theory and practices. If actual practical applications of media production are taught and incorporated within the university or multicultural educational setting, they are often addressed with condescension and allocated to the role of a far less socially credible school employee, usually technical support staff. Such employees are often not interested in or qualified to teach the necessary semiotic skills and analytical concepts of media literacy which must accompany all practical applications of any media form.

Furthermore, the main authority figure, the classroom teacher or professor, often diminishes the importance of this kind of work and/or literacy by the very lack of demonstrated skill and/or interest in learning this form of practical literacy. The teacher thus abdicates to "techies" the pedagogical responsibilities in these arenas. Hence arises the illogical but common practice of blaming the victim, or student in this case, and the technology itself in a fashion that distracts and obscures its potential pedagogical significance. Focusing on the alleged pedagogical harm from media and computer culture diminishes the positive potential of media and technology in society and education, as well as the necessity to become literate in reading and using media and cyberculture.

The computer, as well as the TV set, has now often become a common object of disdain and disrespect within the multicultural educational context. Like the television and Hollywood films that have been blamed by so many educators for educational and human failings among contemporary students, the computer is now also being demonised. Common complaints, used to characterising negative the computer revolution and its associated forums, like the Internet and Web, appear to blame the new technologies, and the student who uses them for playing games like blackjack, or computerised video games. Others complain that students spend too much time on e-mail, in chatrooms, or in web-surfing.

Many educators and critics thus denounce out-of-hand new computer technologies rather than embarking on serious studies of how such tools can be used to enhance multicultural education. In a similar vein, criticisms are also proliferating concerning student propensities toward employing the computer, internet, and the world wide web to plagiarise and cheat on term paper assignments, rather than seriously investigating the ways that computers and multimedia could be productively used to advance research and education. Such criticism obscures the real kinds of epistemological and behavioral shifts that an expanding computer and media culture are producing and the need to develop literacies and pedagogies to make use of these technologies for multicultural educational purposes.

The criticisms often call attention to the challenge and ubiquity of the new technologies and dramatise the need for those who educate and develop multicultural educational curricula to become literate in these domains. Such emergent pedagogical forums deserve the respect with which the written, published word is afforded within the academic and educational realm. All too often, a news story or artifact of media culture depicts youth as taking advantage of the computers in an immoral fashion to access pornography, to cheat, or to play trivial games.

All-too-many educators and critics employ the argument that the new technologies are far more accessible to the privileged and are therefore reinforcing class hierarchies which will eventually enable those children of the predominantly white middle and upper classes to become far more computer literate. Critics often use this argument to imply that computers will generate an even more rigid future of class-based divisions in employment opportunities and social position to denounce computers, rather than devising strategies to make sure that disadvantaged and subordinate groups have access to computer education and technologies.

Merely dismissing computers and new technologies manifests a refusal to confront the need to restructure multicultural education and to cultivate multimedia and computer literacies among all social groups. In fact, the admittedly growing disparity between the haves and have-nots must become part of a media and computer literacy educational epistemology and politics. This cause needs the active participation of educators in political coalitions that seek to make these new technologies more accessible to the underprivileged student populations. Such coalitions require networking teachers and educational professionals with grass-roots organisations, official and unofficial lobby groups, and research and grant organisations. It also requires teachers to become public intellectuals to strive to make schooling responsive to the need to cultivate democratic citizens, as well as relevant to the challenges of a new economy and culture. Overcoming the 'digital divide' thus requires participation in social and educational change to benefit those subordinate groups along the axes of class, gender, and race who have traditionally not received the benefits of ruling social groups.

What is needed therefore is a philosophical and pedagogical shift toward positively deploying new technologies for educational purposes and democratic social transformation. This reconstructive process should seek to empower and enlighten both teachers and students and to assist them in recognising the difference between good and bad, mediocre and beneficial, media and multimedia texts. Teachers and students should learn to evaluate new cultural forms in the same manner in which one judges and evaluates print media material. This approach, however, necessitates a commitment to teaching media, computer, and multimedia literacies and the active incorporation of the best of these programs within the pedagogical forum.

References

Baugh, I. W., Baugh, J. G., "Global classrooms: E-mail learning communities", *Learning and Leading with Technology*, 25 (3), 38-41, 1997.

Cummins, J., Sayers, D., "Multicultural Education and Technology", *Multicultural Education*, 3(3), 4-11, 1996.

Damarin, S. K., "Technology and multicultural education: The question of convergence", *Theory Into Practice*, 37(1), 11-19, 1998.

DeVoogd, G. L., "Computer use levers power sharing: Multicultural students' styles of participation and knowledge", *Computers & Education*, 31(4), 351-364, 1998.

Freedman, K., Liu, M., "The importance of computer experience, learning processes, and communication patterns in multicultural networking", *Educational Technology Research and Development*, 44(1), 43-59, 1996.

Gloria Ladson Billings, *New Directions in Multicultural Education: Complexities, Boundaries, and Critical Race Theory,* University of Wisconsin, Madison

King, J. E., "Culture-centered knowledge: Black studies, curriculum transformation, and social action", In J. A. Banks, C.A.M. Banks Eds., *Handbook of research on multicultural education,* San Francisco: Jossey-Bass, 2001.

Kymlicka, W., (ed.), *The Rights of Minority Cultures,* New York: Oxford University Press, 1995.

Ladson-Billings, G, "Just what is critical race theory and what's it doing in a nice field like education?" *International Journal of Qualitative Studies in Education,* 1998.

Olneck, M., "The recurring dream: Symbolism and ideology in intercultural and multicultural education", *American Journal of Education, 98*(2), 147–174, 1990.

Ravitch, D., "Multiculturalism: E-pluribus plures", *American Scholar,* 59(3), 337–354, 1990.

Roblyer, M.D., Dozier-Henry, O., Burnette, A. P., "Technology and multicultural education: The uneasy alliance", *Educational Technology*, 36(5), 5-12, 1996.

7

Multicultural Education: Creating Educational Equity

Multicultural education came into being where fair-minded people sought ways to respond constructively to the challenge of members of different cultural groups sharing the same society. Although social action for justice may begin in other domains—laws and policies, hiring practices, housing, or access to health care, for example—sooner or later, schools must be involved in the effort. That is because progress in social arrangements ultimately requires that citizens adopt new attitudes, which in turn need new knowledge and experiences.

A new education is needed by people on both sides of the cultural divide. Children of groups who have been oppressed need bolstering; and children of privileged groups need to broaden their perspective to take into account the views of children from other groups. Multicultural education, then, is a movement in schools to promote awareness, mutual appreciation, and harmony among people of different cultural groups—usually with the ultimate goal of achieving social justice and social cohesion.

Multicultural education provides a window into the cultures of minority children, through which children from majority groups can see them accurately. It also provides a mirror of their own culture, to children from minority groups, who heretofore may have seen only negative reflections of themselves, or no reflection at all, in the school curriculum. Admittedly, a few widely scattered exercises in cultural awareness will not go very far to combat years of prejudicial attitudes that have been absorbed at home or in the neighborhood. That is why many experts in multicultural education argue for the infusion of multicultural influences throughout the curriculum and throughout the school day, week, and year.

In fact, approaches that have been taken to multicultural education can be plotted along a continuum from occasional topic lessons to a transformation of the school. In the most straightforward of venues, multicultural education is limited to discussions of school curriculum. From a practical standpoint, this translates into using materials such as children's books, or projects such as oral histories, to increase awareness and understanding of the various cultural perspectives of the students in the school or classroom.

The idea is that the content connects to the child and hence, each child will see himself or herself reflected in the daily curriculum and studies that take place in the classroom. Further, that the class will see itself as a collective made up of different experiences, all of which are equally important and valid, and by doing so will increase the understanding of each child of the other.

Multicultural education is a transformational process that permeates and impacts every aspect of the operation of an educational system, including government policy, staffing, curriculum, disciplinary policy, student involvement, parent and community involvement, pedagogy, assessment, and funding. One of the underlying premises of multicultural education as transformation is "that as schools go so goes the nation," At the practical level, multicultural education then becomes a venue for social and political reform.

Discussions of oppression, social inequality, power dynamics, race and ethnicity, as well as the role of the dominant culture, in the shaping of society's basic assumption about what constitutes school knowledge, appropriate social behaviour, and national identity, is all part of the multicultural education discourse. Regardless of where practice comes down on the definitional continuum, researchers, architects, and practitioners of multicultural education hold certain goals and assumptions in common.

Multicultural education assumes that pluralism is a good thing and that race, ethnicity, cultural and social class are all salient parts of a pluralistic society. Participation in a variety of ethnic experiences ultimately enriches one's understanding of the human experience and leads to a more fulfilling life. A central goal of multicultural education is to help individuals live more productively in a pluralistic society. This is accomplished in two ways:

i) Individuals gain a greater understanding of themselves by seeing themselves through the lens of other cultures.

ii) Individuals gain the necessary skills, knowledge, and attitudes needed to function within their ethnic culture and within and across other ethnic cultures.

Multicultural education is premised on the need for accuracy. In order for individuals to get a true picture of historical and social events, which have shaped national identity, they need to listen to multiple voices and understand multiple perspectives. It is not a matter of leaving out one version of events in favor of another; rather it is about re-envisioning history using an inclusive model that more accurately portrays events as they happened. Multicultural education is a commitment to helping all students master the essential academic and social skills to become knowledgeable, caring, and active citizens in an increasingly polarised and troubled world.

Concepts of Educational Equity

One important goal education is to help all young people aware of the opportunities and expectations that await them in the adult world. To ensure that all students become aware of these opportunities and expectations, schools need to promote and provide students with a fair, effective education within an equitable environment. Schools need to create opportunities; foster skills, knowledge, awareness and understanding; and dispositions for both educators and students to succeed in our diverse and pluralistic state, nation and world. Even though federal and state laws prohibit discrimination, and educators hold a great commitment to providing equal educational opportunities, inequities still exist in our schools. The repercussions from differential treatment or discrimination, often subtle and unintentional rather than overt, are still the same - the individual is shortchanged because of something over which he or she has no control.

The educational policies, practices, and programmes are aimed should:

a) eliminate educational barriers based on gender, race/ ethnicity, national origin, colour, disability, age, or other protected group status; and
b) provide equal educational opportunities and ensure that historically underserved or underrepresented populations meet the same rigorous standards for academic performance expected of all children and youth.

Educational equity knowledge and practices in public schools have evolved over time and require a comprehensive approach. Equity strategies are planned. systemic and focus on the core of the teaching and learning process (curriculum, instruction and school environment/culture)

Educational equity activities promote the real possibility of equality of educational results for each student and between diverse groups of students. The essential dynamic of educational equity is that equity and diversity are a part of every aspect of education. This includes, for example, every plan, every activity, every decision, every class, every policy of the school. The idea of educational equity should permeate everything that happens in the school.

Some of the major educational equity strategies are:

- — Collecting, analysing and using disaggregated assessment data to make educational decisions and establish school improvement efforts.
- — Analysing the intersections of gender, race, culture, disability, class, and sexual orientation that collide to influence teaching and learning.
- — Involving parents and citizens, representative of all the diversity in the community, thereby affirming the growing pluralism that exists.
- — Developing and delivering equitable and inclusive curriculum, extracurricular activities and pupil services.
- — Practicing equitable and inclusive instruction, including detracking, degrouping and reducing differential expectations or treatment of students.
- — Ensuring equitable classroom and school environments in which every student sees their culture authentically and positively portrayed.
- — Providing meaningful professional development opportunities to build capacity for addressing equity and diversity (awareness level to advanced skill building).
- — Improving leadership and administrative practice that enhances equity and diversity.
- — Delivering equitable counseling and guidance, other pupil services, and citizenship experiences which support diversity, expand educational planning and career options, promote resiliency, reduce prejudice and increase self-understanding and positive identity development for all youth.
- — Restructuring school organisations to achieve greater educational equity by changing the roles, rules, and relationships that influence how people work, learn and interact.

— Creating collaborations between school, employers and communities around which opportunities for prejudice reduction respect for diversity and citizenship can occur.

— Promoting equity and nurturing diversity through public information and school organisations and activities.

Principles for achieving Equity and Excellence in Schools

Incorporating the following ten principles permits schools to achieve equity in excellence as an integral element of their structure:

School governance and administration are committed to the integration of equity and excellence. All decision making considers the potential impact on the learning opportunities of all student groups. Publicising disaggregated school data regularly permits comparative monitoring and evaluation of learning opportunities and outcomes by race, national origin, language background, gender, disability and socio-economic status.

Every school programme is accessible to any student who can benefit from participation and is not based on race, national origin, gender, disability or socio-economic status. All students have equal opportunities to make informed choices about programme entry and to prepare adequately for programme participation. Schools and feeder schools meet their shared responsibility to plan for and to prepare students to participate in challenging classes.

All students attend school in a climate of respect, trust and regard that is safe and free from discrimination, bias and harassment. Curriculum content, instructional materials and teaching methods acknowledge and value all students' cultures and languages.

The school has resources adequate to provide all its students with meaningful opportunities to meet the highest learning standards established by the school its district and its state. The resources provide for a satisfactory physical plant and match the needs of the students. All students have equal access to learning equipment and technology.

The curriculum provides a progressive sequence of interdisciplinary, multicultural content aligned with the highest district, state and national content standards. It is active, cumulative and inclusive of all cultures and both genders; it reaches beyond understanding content to the development of skills for evaluating and using information. It includes exposure, instruction and experience in the fine and practical arts of diverse cultures.

The school involves all students in a variety of active, student-centred instructional methods. Instruction fosters independent and cooperative learning, mastery of learning skills, higher order thinking and second languages; it recognises and responds to variety in learning styles, including those which may reflect culture and gender.

The school assesses student learning on a frequent and continuing basis for the primary purpose of improving teaching and learning. Assessments are aligned with learning opportunities, are conducted in a variety of formats, involve the student in self-appraisal, reflect understanding of multiple domains of intelligence and academic learning, and have equal consequences for all students assessed.

The school provides a variety of co-curricular and enrichment activities to meet the academic, vocational and personal interests and needs of all students. It actively encourages the participation of all students and all groups of students and is active in identifying and removing barriers to students' involvement.

The school makes effective partners of the parents of all student groups. It informs parents of education rights, student progress and options; consults them on policy matters; recruits them as cultural and local-history resources; welcomes them as programme volunteers; and consistently involves them in short- and long-range schoolwide planning and Implementation.

The school is an important link in a school-community network that supports a safe, caring environment of continuing and stimulating experience for children. It provides early educational services; provides or collaborates with daycare programmes; provides parenting programmes for community adults; and it collaborates with community agencies and groups through referrals for health, social, recreational and cultural programmes and services.

Programme Development

In the multicultural education movement, there are some general models and specific areas of research that offer educators and policy makers a road map for programme development.

Content-Oriented Programmes

Content-oriented programmes are the most easily recognisable and hence the most common form of multicultural education. Content-oriented programmes are committed to the inclusion of material that reflects the cultural make-up of the class or the school. The primary goal of these programmes is to make students more knowledgeable about cultures within their schools or their communities.

Content-oriented programmes come in various levels of engagement and infusion of the curriculum. It gives only a cursory nod to multicultural education by focusing solely on "heroes and holiday". Students would read books, do projects, and learn about a variety of holidays but through the lens of the standard canon. At this stage, multicultural education is an add-on or tangential to current curriculum without changing the actual focus. More sophisticated and complex programmes, however, set out to actually transform the curriculum. These programmes have three goals:

i) to develop multicultural content across the disciplines

ii) to incorporate a variety of different viewpoints and perspectives in the curriculum

iii) to transform the canon, ultimately developing a new paradigm for the curriculum

Student-Oriented Programmes

Student-oriented programmes address the academic and learning needs of carefully defined groups of students, most specifically minority students. The goal of these programmes is often to raise the academic achievement of these groups. Research in learning styles, language use and development, etc., often forms the basis of these programmes. Since the goal of student-oriented programmes is to improve the academic success of specific groups and thereby make it possible for them to enter the mainstream, they are often seen as compensatory in nature. Further, there is no particular guarantee that student-oriented programmes will be done in conjunction with content oriented programmes.

Socially-Oriented Programmes

Socially-oriented programmes are generally the most inclusive and broad-based. They are also often controversial and as a consequence less common. Programmes such as these attempt to reform "both the schooling and the cultural and political contexts of schooling". The over-arching goal of socially-oriented programmes is to increase cultural and racial tolerance and reduce bias as well as rearrange the social structure to reinforce and support this new paradigm. In order to accomplish this, socially-oriented programmes have a number of distinguishing characteristics:

i) They seek to revise and transform the curriculum to create a new canon that is reflective of the current society.

ii) They seek to use current educational research to discover new ways to engage students in the educational enterprise in order that they may be academically successful, regardless of ethnicity and class.

iii) They use the instruments and strategies of social activism and community organisation to accomplish these goals.

iv) They focus on the outcome of preparing students to be socially—active citizens and agents of change.

As a consequence, such programmes use a variety of approaches borrowed from disciplines as diverse as philosophy, ecology, and psychology. Some programmes emphasise critical thinking and critical discourse, collaborative learning and multilingualism.

Cultural Standard and Educational Equity

There are now new demands since educators feel they have to respond to the students' learning needs and expectations related to linguistic and cultural diversity. In order to illustrate some of these changes, we have chosen three innovations in three different areas of intervention: the postulation of standards or indicators of good culturally sensitive pedagogical practice, the preparation and distribution of educational materials attempting to recognise and incorporate local knowledge and cultural beliefs and practices *vis-a-vis* western style curriculum content and the education of teachers, both at pre-service and inservice levels, in skills related to communication, mediation and conflict resolution in a multicultural setting.

Education departments of many countries has been developing "content standards" to define what students should know and be able to do as they go through school. In addition, "performance standards" are being developed for teachers and administrators, as well as a set of "quality school standards" to serve as a basis for accrediting schools. To the extent that these standards are written for general use, they don't always address some of the special issues that are of critical importance to schools in rural area, particularly for those serving native communities and students.

Within such a setting and through a series of regional and state-wide meetings, the native educators can develop standards to provide a way for schools and communities to examine the extent to which they are attending to the educational and cultural well being of the students in their care. These "cultural standards" are predicated in the belief that a form of education grounded in the heritage language and culture indigenous to a particular place is a fundamental prerequisite associated with that place, and thus is an essential ingredient for identifying the appropriate qualities and practices associated with culturally responsive educators, curriculum and schools.

Though the emphasis of these standards is on rural schools serving native communities, many of them are applicable to all students and communities because they focus curricular attention on an indepth study of the surrounding and cultural environment in which the school is situated, while recognising the unique contribution that indigenous people can make to such study as long-term inhabitants who have accumulated extensive specialised knowledge related to that environment. Standards have been drawn up in five areas, including those for students, educators, curriculum, schools and communities.

These "cultural standards" provide guidelines or touchstones against which schools and communities can examine what they are doing to attend to the cultural well being of the young people they are responsible for nurturing to adulthood. While the state-standards stipulate what all students should know and be able to do, the cultural standards are oriented more towards providing guidance on how to get them there in such a way that they become responsible, capable and whole human beings in the process.

The emphasis is on fostering a strong connection between what students experience in school and their lives out of school by providing opportunities for students to engage in indepth experiential learning in real-world contexts. The focus in the curriculum is shifted from teaching and learning about cultural heritage as another subject to teaching and learning through the local culture as a foundation for all education. It is intended that all forms of knowledge, ways of knowing and worldviews be recognised as equally valid, adaptable and complementary to one another in mutually beneficial ways.

The cultural standards are not intended to be inclusive, exclusive and conclusive, and thus should be reviewed and adapted to fit specific local needs. Neither are they supposed to produce standardisation, but rather to encourage schools to nurture and build upon the rich and varied cultural traditions that continue to be practised in communities . Some of the multiple uses to which these cultural standards may be put are the following:

i) As a basis for reviewing school or district-level goals, policies and practices with regard to the curriculum and pedagogy being implemented.
ii) To devise locally appropriate ways to review student and teacher performance.
iii) To strengthen the commitment to revitalising the local language and culture and fostering the involvement of elders as an educational resource.
iv) As criteria against which to evaluate educational programmes intended to address the cultural needs of students.

In relation to curriculum development, a culturally-responsive curriculum should:

i) Reinforce the integrity of the cultural knowledge that students bring with them;
ii) Recognise cultural knowledge as part of a living and constantly adapting system that is grounded in the past, but continues to grow through the present and into the future;
iii) Use the local language and cultural knowledge as a foundation for the rest of the curriculum;

iv) Foster a complementary relationship across knowledge derived from diverse knowledge systems.

v) Situate local knowledge and actions in a global context.

Testing and Assessment

School assessment purposes other than for achievement have been ranking, classification and placement of students, for treatment in special education and or school tracks. A small number of psychologists and special educators also claimed to be doing diagnostic testing and assessment. During these decades there have been fundamental conceptual changes in the science and academics of testing and assessment. One of the most interesting is the cognitive change approach. Another set of changes has been the acceptance of the underdevelopment of the field of mental measurement by experts, and the development of a vision of possibilities. In spite of these conceptual changes for a significant number of scientists, there have been far fewer changes in professional practices among the overwhelming majority of professionals in applied psychology in education.

Where the 'equity problem' in testing and assessment in education for minority cultural groups is concerned, It will be seen that these groups are the canaries in the miner's cap signalling deep problems with the whole enterprise of mass produced standardised testing and assessment, a paradigm problem. Cultural anthropologists and experts from other related academic disciplines can inform the work of psychometrics and the assessments that are linked to that work. When applied to minority ethnic groups in a cultural and political environment, simple assessment practice problems can be magnified.

Validity in Testing and Assessment

Common types of validity in testing and assessment are:

i) construct validity,

ii) face validity,

iii) content validity,

iv) concurrent validity, and

v) predictive validity.

By far, predictive validity, or forecasting, is valued most, with "intelligence" and cognitive testing. In general, predictive validity rests on the assumption of fixed abilities, resulting in the expectation that students will maintain their approximate rank in a distribution of scores of "mental ability".

The various validities were applied in different proportions to "cognitive" or "intelligence" testing and to "achievement" testing, collectively the primary forms of school testing. Of course, "personality", "interest" and other types of testing were sometimes used to a lesser degree.

For the most part in practice, testing includes little "assessment" or problem solving. There are few rigorous and commonly accepted standards for "assessment" as there are with testing. The romantic notion that many sources of valid data are combined with testing, and integrated in an instructionally valid way in school practice, simply has not been documented.

The standardised routines that have been executed were accepted, on faith, as important activities to support, implicitly and rarely explicitly, beneficial school services. Gradually, some psychologists and educators began to be concerned about alternative meanings and values of the testing/assessment enterprise in schools. A few took action to develop approaches based on a new paradigm. However, even today, testing and assessment activities tend to be compliance activities, not to be confused with activities that inform instructionally valid design.

Three decades ago, there was not even a hint of a substantial challenge to the accepted idea of standardised, mass-produced, "one-size fits-all" assessment for all children, or that it would be beneficial universally for any students. Culture was ignored or minimised as a factor in creating testing routines, or in interpreting testing and assessment data. Students' economic opportunity and what we now call "opportunities to learn" were also ignored. Most responses to the challenge of cultural deficiencies in testing and assessment tended to be political.

Some educators and psychologists have argued for "equity" in testing and assessment, for "culture free", "culturally fair", and "culturally relevant" or "culturally salient" testing and assessment. There is also "non-discriminatory" testing and assessment that speaks to equity without specific mention of culture. This equity oriented and intuitive response to the validity problem fell far short of what was needed, mainly because the assessment problem is not really understood as a validity problem, as a matter of science.

No scientifically based data have been collected routinely on "opportunity-to-learn", "non-discrimination" and "cultural" factors to be included in the assessment. No standards have been developed to demonstrate the scientific basis for such adjustments.

The doubts about the validity of testing and assessment are not new. Some of the early pioneers were clear about the limitations of standardised testing. Existing instruments (for measuring intellect) represent enormous improvements over what was available twenty years ago, but three fundamental defects remain. Just what they measure is not known, how far it is proper to add, subtract, multiply, divide, compute ratios with the measures obtained is not known; just what the measures obtained signify concerning intellect is not known. We may refer to these defects in order as ambiguity in content, arbitrariness in units, and ambiguity in significance. Unfortunately, the testing movement seems to be propelled by inertia. It has not been able to hear and to respond appropriately to the other scientific information that would have a major bearing on the work of psychologists.

Validity, requires taking such variables as culture and opportunity-to-learn into account. These things matter greatly in testing and assessment, and in the delivery of instructional services to students. Context includes culture and socio-economic status. The research community, belatedly within the past decade, recognises contextual variables as influential. These variables pose great threats to standardised mass-produced testing and assessment validity, especially in the absence of controls for context variation in validation studies. They also pose a great challenge to profits from mass production. It must be noted that typical validation studies of IQ tests are correlational and not experimental.

Instructional validity

The foundation academic disciplines for the support of education have been psychology, sociology, and anthropology to a lesser extent. When we move beyond day-to-day school instructional services, disciplines such as economics, business, and other areas contribute to policy studies. What is interesting about all of these disciplines, and especially about psychology (testing and assessment), is that until very recently, there was no explicit benefits criterion for the evaluation of instruction and the testing and assessment practices that inform instruction. In other words, for example, psychology, the primary testing and assessment discipline, was not evaluated in terms of its contribution to beneficial instruction, only in terms of the faithful execution of psychological procedures or routines and recipes. Under current job descriptions, school psychologists take no responsibility for powerful instruction, only forecasting student performance.

The traditional validity criteria for "mental measurement" did not include empirically determined "instructional validity", the linking of testing and assessment to the improvement of instructional outcomes. Some psychometric experts refer to this as "consequential validity". To name "instructional validity" is to set in motion activities to provide empirical documentation to determine if it exists.

Instructionally valid beneficial testing and assessment approaches have been available for more than half a century. However, it comes from an entirely different paradigm, a marginalised paradigm. This alternative paradigm, rooted in the cognitive psychology of Binet and Piaget, assumes malleable intelligence, and demonstrates the instructional validity of diagnostic cognitive assessment and remedial teaching or mediation. The diagnostic assessment is called "dynamic assessment" for structural cognitive modifiability. The remedial teaching is called "instrumental enrichment" for changing cognitive structures in an enduring way. The goal is to assess the student's mental perceptions, definitions, functions, operations and structures.

In other words, cognitive processes are of greater interest than the acquisition of cognitive content. Further, the uses of the process information must be beneficial for instruction. The remedial paradigm changes the assumptions, the questions, the goals, the roles of professionals, and many other things. This approach, although marginalised, does show powerful achievement benefits for students. A brief word is in order here about achievement testing. The primary concern about achievement testing is that tests be "content valid". It is not rocket science to say that tests should measure what schools promise to teach. Of course, in the real world, students rarely are exposed to a common curriculum with a uniformly high quality of professional service. Rarely do valid tests exist of the actual curriculum that is offered, the actual opportunities to learn. Time and time again, empirical work demonstrates the lack of content validity of popularly used standardised tests. Empirical documentation of the "Savage Inequalities" in opportunities-to-learn in school services offered to students is abundant.

Since few curricula are culturally salient, few tests are either. Cultural salience is of great importance, since students should have the opportunity to demonstrate what they know and can do; in perceptions, operations, functions and structures, using cultural material that is familiar to them. In addition, the human experience is an enormously diverse experience. The truth of the human experience must be reflected in the diversity of the school world. Any non-diverse curriculum is an untruthful one, be that a curriculum in mathematics, science, art, music, history, etc. Mass produced standardised achievement tests have a poor content validity track record. That will remain a problem because savage inequalities in opportunities-to-learn shows no signs of abating.

Standardised mass produced tests are not measurement when applied in the world of diversity. This means that they must be taken for what they are—rough instruments for data gathering as a point of departure for assessment. They may give some indication of the results of exposure to instruction. Some of these data may be useful, potentially even beneficial.

Testing and assessment are dependent upon communication systems that are tied to language. Language is culturally embedded and is a core part of the communication process. Cultural linguists are scientists who have developed a body of knowledge and models of meaning that are essential to the work of those who use language in making measurement devices and in the interpretation of the meaning of mediation and responses.

Standardisation

Standardisation in testing and assessment is of high value to entrepreneurs, who make money, if they can mass-produce products, such as tests. The best of all possible worlds for them is "one size fits all." Unfortunately for their needs, humanity made up of a plurality of cultures. Until now, it is rare to see any academic/scientific expertise in culture, its contents and principles, reflected in mainstream psychology.

The reality of cultural diversity and its meaning for science is often seen by measurement experts as a "minority concern", a "fairness concern", a "civil rights concern", an "equity concern", but not a scientific concern. This means that many scholars, often noting the concerns above, seem to believe that cultural diversity matters are more political than scientific. Moreover, there is real resistance among many traditional psychologists to engage in the required scientific study and dialogue about these cultural matters. Their cultural naivete is almost legendary. The field of psychology is littered with the wreckage of attempts to function professionally in ignorance of cultural realities, and in ignorance of the cultural sciences that document and interpret those realities.

Managing Diversity

As our society has changed from an industrial society concerned with nationalism and uniformity, to an information society concerned with internationalism and diversity, on the way to the global society of the twenty-first century concerned with the environment and interconnectedness, the ethnic make-up of society as well as of our schools has also changed. Such cultural and political upheavals have given rise to knowledgeable players in the game of social change, while leaving most people as confused bystanders, desperately hanging on to a past which in part is dysfunctional to the present and in many ways irrelevant to the future.

The needs of the twenty-first century demand a citizenry that is culturally sensitive and internationally focused, with an orientation toward the future rather than the past. Multiculturalism, as the new paradigm for education for our century, is a political ping-pong term greatly misused and highly misunderstood. Since for many it is also a value-ladened concept, it has come under fire from diverse segments of the population, who due to their social position view the world differently. The fact that where you stand determines what you see is a reality in most situations, and it is especially true for the concept of multiculturalism.

Multiculturalism is a system of beliefs and behaviours that recognises and respects the presence of all diverse groups in an organisation or society, acknowledges and values their socio-cultural differences, and encourages and enables their continued contribution within an inclusive cultural context which empowers all within the organisation or society.

The change, brought about by the multiculturalism, is putting pressure on the old structures of the educational system and of society. And unless these old brittle structures are willing to make the necessary changes, the result will be social spillage—protests, disturbances, apathy, dropouts, a lack of financial support from the community, and a voting with the feet as parents take their children elsewhere to private schools.

Managing diversity is an on-going process that unleashes the various talents and capabilities which a diverse population bring to an organisation, community or society, so as to create a wholesome, inclusive environment, that is "safe for differences", enables people to "reject rejection", celebrates diversity, and maximises the full potential of all, in a cultural context where everyone benefits.

Multiculturalism, as the art of managing diversity, is an *inclusive* process where no one is left out. Diversity, in its essence, then is a 'safeguard against idolatry'—the making of one group as the norm for all groups. Therefore, one of the dangers that must be avoided in grasping a proper understanding of multiculturalism is *bashism*.

Bashism is the tendency to verbally and/or physically attack another person or group based solely on the negative meaning given to group membership—due to biological, cultural, political or socioeconomic differences (such as gender, age, race/ethnicity, political party, class, education, values, religious affiliation or sexual orientation)—without regard for the individual. The motivating factor for bashism is fear, arising out of ignorance of the other.

One of the backwashes of a narrow view of multiculturalism, especially as espoused by some women and persons of color, is called as "white maleism". White Maleism is the tendency of minority groups to blame white males for most of the social evil in the world today, especially as it relates to sexism and racism, and view them as selfish, ruthless, unrepentant and unredeemable, and, as a consequence, refuse to recognise and accept the contribution that many white males have made, continue to make, and desire to make, to remove oppression.

While much of oppression today has been the historical by-product of the abuse of power by white males, not much is gained in terms of creating an inclusive, caring, compassionate educational system and society, by reversing the process and excluding many white males who have been instrumental in creating the "house of abundance" and structures of inclusion.

Some of us persons of colour would not be where we are today if it were not for culturally, politically and morally concerned white males who opened institutional doors, made decisions, implemented policies, and stood in the breach to bridge the gulf of intolerance. The effective management of diversity includes, empowers and benefits all persons concerned, whites included.

In an age of cultural pluralism, multiculturalism is needed to manage diversity effectively. In essence, then, multiculturalism is nothing more than the art of managing diversity in a total quality manner. It is the only option open to educators, leaders and administrators in an ever-increasing culturally pluralistic environment. In schools the process of multiculturalism is best maintained through

Multicultural education is an intrinsic approach to education and curriculum construction that acknowledges and respects the contributions which the various racial/ethnic groups have made to society, and incorporates these contributions in an overall programme of instruction which meets the needs of an ever-changing society and is sensitive to the personal and social development of all persons concerned. Today's diverse student populations and workforce is simply not going to go away, but increase. This is the direction of the future—multicultural, multiethnic, multilingual communities. And effective leaders, concerned with the bottom line—the maximising of profit, whether material or nonmaterial—are recognising this new direction.

The art of managing diversity is thus of great concern to all persons charged with the responsibility of overseeing the work of others. Organisations, however, that try to force today's reality into yesterday's management styles will seriously jeopardise the viability of their enterprise. Beyond the challenge of creating a humane educational environment where students and staff of diverse backgrounds and experiences learn to appreciate each other, lies the additional one of changing the structural arrangements.

Managing diversity should be a comprehensive, holistic process for developing an environment that works for all concerned. There are two dimensions to a holistic model of managing diversity—horizontal and vertical. The first, focused on the individual, is concerned with the horizontal dimension of embracing and valuing differences. This area is of tremendous importance, since individual students and staff that do not get along, nor understand each other, are not able to maximise their greatest potential for optimal excellence. Here is where workshops on prejudice, cultural awareness, cross-cultural communication and conflict resolution are most helpful. However, if this is all that is done such efforts will come to naught, for the individual interactional dimension is only one dimension of change.

The purpose of valuing diversity and appreciating differences is not simply to make people feel good about each other. Schools have a specific purpose for existing, to implement their mission through whatever product or service they provide. Thus, bringing interactional change at the individual level is only half the process. Such change must be paralleled by a change in the culture and structure of the school, the vertical dimension, since it is here where the root problems at the horizontal level often reside.

Many schools and organisations regard themselves as "multicultural" simply on the basis of the ethnic diversity present in their midst. But is this what makes an organisation multicultural? And if not, what does and what are the implications for effective schools in the twenty-first century? The mere presence of an ethnically and racially diverse student population, due to legal, moral or social imperatives, does not make a school multicultural This is merely being concerned with affirmative action. This was the main accomplishment of the 1960s and 1970s, giving people access to the system. In the 1980s the concern was with "valuing differences". In the 1990s the push is for "managing diversity." But in the twenty-first century the focus of schools and corporations needs to be on "living diversity".

Many schools and organisations, however, have begun to go back on affirmative action, instead of going on to living diversity. What this means is that the number of ethnically diverse students sitting in the classrooms does not make a school multicultural. All that this may simply represent is that students have gained access to the school—they've gotten through the front door. But if all a school does is to give access, then students may leave just as quickly out the back door.

Neither is it merely a concern for understanding, respecting, valuing and celebrating the differences among the various groups represented in the school. Valuing diversity is important, as it may engender an awareness of and a sensitivity to differences, but it does not necessarily translate into structural changes.

The factors that make a school multicultural are its :

— Perspectives
— Policies
— Programmes
— Personnel
— Practices

To make a school multicultural, implement the following imperatives:

— Reflect the heterogeneity of the school—the dynamic of Affirmative Action;
— Are sensitive to the needs of the various groups comprising the student population—the dynamic of Valuing Differences;

— Incorporate their contributions to the overall mission of the school—the dynamic of Managing Diversity;

— Create a cultural and social ambiance that is inclusive and empowers all groups in the school—the dynamic of Living Diversity.

These four imperatives form the basis of multicultural education. This is an approach to education and curriculum construction that acknowledges and respects the contributions which the various racial/ethnic groups have made to society, and incorporates these contributions in an overall programme of instruction which meets the needs of an ever-changing society and is sensitive to the personal and social development of all persons concerned.

At the heart of what makes a school multicultural lies managing diversity—the proper management of the diversity in a school for the empowerment of all groups, which includes changing mindsets as well as the underlying culture of a school, especially if this culture is what is impeding change, in order for the school to begin living diversity so as to more effectively accomplish its mission. This is what makes a school multicultural. The point behind this is that unity in diversity needs to be the basic premise of all that is done in education. This is where the five factors come into play, because the rapid changes taking place in society are forcing schools to move away from a lethargic business-as-usual, reactive mindset, to a proactive one that anticipates and implements change.

Perspectives refers to the vision without which education as well as schools perish. Vision is the bifocal ability to see what lies ahead (farsightedness), as well as the various impediments in the present (nearsightedness), and how to avoid them in order to arrive at the future. It must be bifocal, for focus on the future at the expense of the present, or vice versa, will result in loss and in a detour in the mission of the school. A sense of vision and mission, will lead to appropriate *Policies*, the guarantees that make known the intents of the school. Policies give rise to *Programmes* that put in action what education is all about. But effective programmes cannot be run without the right *Personnel*, reflective of the diversity in the school. The last one is *Practices*, the actual conduct of the school, its staff and administration.

Of the five factors, the most important one is the "practices". A school may have the best perspectives, policies, programmes, and personnel, but these are only cosmetic until practiced. And it only takes a small number of personnel who in their practice refuse to go along with a programme or fail to implement policy, for an otherwise well designed plan to be sabotaged. The five factors have to alter present school structures and cultures, especially if these are exclusive and do not benefit everyone in the school.

Multicultural education will enable administrators, teachers and their students to become world citizens—persons who are able to transcend their own racial/ethnic, gender, cultural and socio-political reality and identify with humankind throughout the world, at all levels of human need. They are thus a transcending people who know no boundaries, and whose operating life-principle is compassion. This is the principle that should be modeled in our schools by the faculty, students, staff and administrators, in the process of living diversity. The challenge is great but so is the reward. This area of change, focused on the institution, is concerned with the vertical dimension of harnessing and empowering diversity, the area that deals with school culture and structure, the way tasks are divided to accomplish the mission of the school.

This dimension holds the key to effecting the greatest change in a school, for it is here where exclusion finds it most comfortable home. But change must be more than merely cosmetic, such as adding a diverse looking population to the school. It must also examine in what ways the vision, values, mission and structure of the school contribute or undermine effective utilisation of the assets all persons bring to an school. Change at both of these dimensions results in cultural inclusion at the center, where living diversity takes place.

This holistic model of managing diversity is called Total Quality Diversity. Total Quality Diversity (TQD) is a holistic model of managing diversity that operates on two levels: The Horizontal—the individual interactional change dimension (embracing and valuing diversity); and the Vertical—the institutional structural change dimension (harnessing and empowering diversity). Both factors are driven by the bottom line profit motive, to help institutions such as schools deliver a quality product—students prepared to meet human needs in a competitive world society.

Diversity has two dimensions, the primary (mainly biological, usually visible: age, gender, race, ethnicity, sexual orientation, disabilities), and the secondary (sociocultural, usually invisible: language, education, values occupation, culture, learning sty, etc.). These various differences that inhibit inclusion at both the individual and institutional dimensions, need to be examined in light of the goal of schools and communities to begin "living diversity". This is an approach to education and communal life that views multiculturalism as integral to the very fabric of our culture, as a basic value undergirding all that is done.

Total Quality Respect (TQR) is an integral part of Total Quality Diversity, in that the proper management of today's diverse schools is not possible without respect for human beings. TQR is the process whereby the other is treated with deference, courtesy and compassion in an endeavor to safeguard the integrity, dignity, value and social worth of the individual. It means treating people the way they want to be treated. It is a lack of respect for others, no matter their position or the differences they bring to an institution, which gives rise to most of the conflicts in organisations.

Organisations are unlikely to embark on change initiatives unless they either are experiencing pain regarding diversity issues, or lack a vision of the challenges before them. Both factors are driven by the bottom line profit motive, to help organisations deliver a quality product or service that meets human needs in a competitive society. The main objective of the holistic model of managing diversity is to accomplish this motive. The end result of this Total Quality Diversity process of management is a lean, competitive organisation, with a multicultural, truly diverse student body/workforce, where creativity, imagination, and intelligence operate in a democratic classroom, workplace and environment.

The key dynamic in diversity management then is to maintain the two dimensions of unity and diversity in balanced tension, without erring to either side. Erring on the side of unity results in uniformity and sameness at the expense of our human uniqueness and distinctiveness. Erring on the side of diversity magnifies differences and separation at the expense of our common, shared humanity.

Unity is not synonymous with uniformity, neither is diversity synonymous with separation. The solution to the tension is to respect and value diversity while working for unity, otherwise exclusion is the result. Thus the strength of a nation or organisation lies in unity in diversity.

References

Dandy, Evelyn B., *Black Communications: Breaking Down the Barriers*, Chicago: African American Images, 1991.

Delpit, Lisa and Dowdy, Jo Ann (eds.), *The Skin We Speak: Thoughts on Language and Culture in the Classroom*, New York: New Press, 2002.

Donovan, M. Suzanne and Cross, Christopher T., *Minority Students in Special and Gifted Education, Commission on Minority Representation in Special and Gifted Education, Behavioural and Social Sciences and Education,* National Research Council, Washington, DC: National Academy Press, 2001.

Hehir, Thomas and Latus, Thomas, "Special Education at Century's End: Evaluation of Theory and Practice Since 1970", *Harvard Educational Review Reprint Series,* Number 23,1992 .

Heller, Kirby A., Holtzman, Wayne H., and Messick, Samuel (eds.), *Placing Children in Special Education: A Strategy for Equity,* Washington, DC: National Academy Press, 1982.

Kozol, Jonathan Savage, *Inequalities: Children in America's Schools*, New York: Crown, 1991.

Lidz, Carol and Elliott, Julian G. (eds.), *Dynamic Assessment: Theory, Models, and Applications*, New York: Pantheon Books, 2000.

______________ , *Dynamic Assessment: Prevailing Models and Applications*, New York: JAI, An Imprint of Elsevier Science, 2000.

8

Multiculturalism and Promises of Pedagogy

Multicultural education relates to education and instruction designed for the cultures of several different races in an educational system. This approach to teaching and learning is based upon consensus building, respect, and fostering cultural pluralism within racial societies. Multicultural education acknowledges and incorporates positive racial idiosyncrasies into classroom atmospheres.

The 1990s witnessed a significant demographic transformation among world nations. In United States, over 30 per cent of school age population were children of colour in 2000. Researches indicated that ethnic minority students are disproportionately poor, dropping out of school, being suspended or expelled, and achieving far below their potential relative to the ethnic majority. Consequently, teachers must prepare themselves and their children for the ever changing challenge of interacting and communicating with diverse races. Reduction of fear, ignorance, and personal detachment are possible benefits to a multicultural education.

With integrated curriculum, social activities, administrative support, and staff training, fear, ignorance, and personal detachment may be notably reduced in both students and teachers. Benefits to multicultural education can help to eliminate the crux of stereotyping, prejudice, racism, and bigotry. If people are to embrace diversity, the conscious and unconscious expressions of racism within our society must be identified and done away with. Multicultural education is the potential catalyst to bring all races together in harmony.

According to some views, if one wants to alienate and further fragment the communication and rapport between ethnic groups, implement multicultural education. As stated by Bennett, "to dwell on cultural differences is to foster negative prejudices and stereotypes, and that is human nature to view those who are different as inferior". Thus, multicultural education will enhance feelings of being atypical. Schools may see multicultural education as a way to "colour blind" their students to differences. Administrators may view the "colour blind" approach as a gate keeper that assures equal treatment and justice for all students and as a way to facilitate compatibility and sameness of all cultures. A common statement from this line of thinking is, 'we are more alike than different'.

Over time, multicultural education may have unplanned for and undesired consequences. It rejects the historic goals of assimilation and integration of ethnic cultures into the majority culture. Ot may increase the resentment encountered by students who feel that changes in school traditions, curriculum, and academic standards are not necessary to get along and respect students from ethnic minorities. Since many institutions resist change of any kind, passive resistance on the part of the administration may simulate acceptance of the tenants of multicultural education.

The concept of multicultural education has probably been as often misunderstood and misused as the idea of equity. Just the term multicultural education means different things to different people. This confusion has arisen, in part, because the phrase is presumed to be understood by everyone, and because it is often mistaken for similar terms which are used interchangeably, among them intercultural, cross-cultural, global, and multi-ethnic.

To school administrators who are concerned with providing equal opportunities to their students, multicultural education has often meant meeting legal guidelines. Some teachers have regarded multicultural education as an additive programme, one that offers culture-specific activities, while others have regarded multicultural education as a subtractive programme, with pull-out components such as ESL classes. To students, multicultural education may have meant meeting a foreign student and learning about his or her culture.

Whatever the rubric, multicultural education has emerged as a response to social and historical events throughout the world, and this type of educational opportunity has been targeted at improving issues of racism, discrimination, prejudice, and social differentiation while better preparing the student for post-school experiences in an increasingly global community. However, rather than being seen as the antidote for all social problems by adding and subtracting educational programmes, multicultural education must be viewed as central to the understanding of why and how these issues persist, and must be addressed across the curriculum.

Sensitivity to other cultures, knowledge of their viewpoints, and accurate assessments of similarities and differences among peoples of the world are vital to preparing students for life in a diversified society. These guidelines, designed to move the multicultural agenda forward and, in so doing, create a positive school climate for all students, is not intended to suggest that we can rid ourselves of all of the biases that colour our judgments or the bias of our own perceptual valuing.

The ultimate goal is to provide a beginning toward the recognition and acceptance of individual and cultural diversity. Further, these guidelines have been written to bring about self-awareness of one's own cultural background and to enable all children to bring those experiences to the multicultural table.

Multicultural education is interdisciplinary, cross-curricular education which prepares students to live, learn, and work together to achieve common goals in a culturally diverse world. It does this by:

— enabling all students to be aware of and affirmed in their own cultural roots;

— allowing all students to understand and value diversity, fostering appreciation, respect, and understanding for persons of different backgrounds; and

— preparing students to live fruitful lives in an increasingly global society with shifting and permeable borders.

The goal of multicultural education is to maximise the potential of all students regardless of race, cultural heritage, sex, or disability. The multicultural education plan, materials, and instructional strategy should provide equal opportunity to all and result in positive outcomes for males and females in all racial and cultural groups. School site staff, in conjunction with district personnel, must take responsibility for providing the materials and assistance necessary to ensure that instruction in all disciplines is accurate, comprehensive, nonbiased, and inclusive of a variety of perspectives.

Multicultural education is a process, not a product, and must be infused throughout the entire educational structure, including: curriculum design; in-school and extracurricular activities; school-based decision making councils; textbook and curricular materials review and selection; and recruitment and retention of minority teachers and staff.

Multicultural education will not benefit just one group of students at the expense of others. All students, regardless of race, national origin, gender, disability, or religion need to see themselves reflected in the curriculum and the entire educational structure in a realistic and positive way. In addition to providing a basis for a positive self concept among all students, including minorities, girls, and students with disabilities, multicultural education helps to prevent a false sense of superiority which often leads to prejudice and discriminatory behavior in later life. Given the mobility in present society and the ever-increasing interdependence among peoples and nations, the lack of minority group representation in the community and/or school is not a valid reason for failing to implement a multicultural education programme.

Education for a Globalised World

The process of globalisation becomes a more immediate reality for the planet's population. Economic globalisation brings the producers and the consumers of different continents and regions into functional relationship with each other. Today's global corporations are organised in such a fashion that a single product may contain parts made in dozens of factories in as many different countries. The managers and employees of these giant firms often spend more time shuttling between countries than they do at home with family and friends, rather like the soldiers of fortune of olden times.

The rapid expansion of communications networks, especially the audiovisual media, has brought what used to be considered unrelated events in faraway places into the intimate space of millions of homes from metropolitan neighbourhoods to urban slums to remote villages. The exotic is no longer distant and the distant becomes ever more familiar. To the extent that the cultural industries promote the lifestyles of the Western, urbanindustrial, middle-class sectors by way of satellite dishes and video stores, the multicultural world draws closer together, and the cultural values of those lifestyles become, as it were, international standards against which local populations measure their achievements and aspirations.

The counterpoint to globalisation is reflected in the massive movements of populations across international borders. Whereas in earlier times colonial settlers spread out from Europe into the so-called undeveloped areas, in recent decades millions upon millions of migrant workers and their families have flocked into the industrial heartlands of Europe and North America from all over the former colonies and the economic periphery, in search of better livelihoods and, frequently, to escape oppressive political and social conditions as well. Even as the former industrial economies are in fact 'de-industrialising' and exporting many of their manufacturing operations abroad, massive migrations of culturally diverse peoples from Third World countries impose increasing strains on traditional labour markets and the social fabric of the host countries.

Most modern nation-states are organised on the assumption that they are, or should be, culturally homogeneous. That is the essence of modern 'nationhood', upon which contemporary statehood and citizenship are founded. No matter that in most cases the facts differ from the model; nowadays, mono-ethnic states are the exception rather than the rule. But the idea of the mono-ethnic, culturally homogeneous nation has been used more often than not to disguise the fact that such states are more adequately described as ethnocratic, that is, where a single majority or dominant ethnic group manages to impose its own vision of 'nationhood' upon the rest of society.

In such circumstances, ethnic groups that do not conform to the dominant model are treated as 'minorities', not only numerically, but mainly in sociological and political terms. This contradiction leads not infrequently to social tensions and conflicts that have escalated in recent years in a number of countries. Indeed, many of the current ethnic conflicts in the world can be traced to the problems inherent in the way the modern nation-state manages ethnic diversity within its borders. Those problems are directly reflected in the social, cultural and educational policies adopted by states with regard to the various peoples, nations and ethnic groups that live within their borders.

One of the most important roles assigned to formal schooling in many countries has been to fashion good, law-abiding citizens who will share a single national identity and who will be loyal to the nation-state. Whilst this no doubt served a noble purpose, and may even have been necessary in certain historical circumstances, it also led in many instances to the marginalisation and even the destruction of numerous ethnically distinct peoples whose cultures, religions, languages, beliefs or ways of life did not conform to the so-called national ideal.

Religious, linguistic and national minorities, as well as indigenous and tribal peoples were often subordinated, sometimes forcefully and against their will, to the interests of the state and the dominant society. While many people thus acquired a new identity and national consciousness, others had to discard their own cultures, languages, religions and traditions, and adapt to the alien norms and customs that were consolidated and reproduced through national institutions, including the education and legal systems.

In many countries there are tensions between the purposes and requirements of a 'national' system of education, and the values, interests and aspirations of culturally distinct peoples. At the same time, in an increasingly interdependent world, conflicting tendencies pull in different directions: on the one hand, the trend toward national homogenisation and world uniformisation; on the other, the search for roots, community and distinctiveness, which for some can only be found by strengthening local and regional identities, and keeping a healthy distance from the 'others', who are sometimes perceived as threatening.

Such a complex situation represents a challenge to the education system and to state-sponsored cultural policies, as well as to the functioning of market mechanisms in the fields of communications and entertainment, those vast networks in which global cultural industries call the shots. In recent years, traditional educational policies based on the premise of a single national culture have come under increasing critical scrutiny.

More and more states not only tolerate expressions of cultural diversity but now recognise that instead of being an obstacle to be overcome, multicultural and pluri-ethnic populations are the true mainstays of democratic social integration. Education in the twenty-first century must come to grips with that challenge, and education systems must be flexible and imaginative enough to be able to strike a creative balance between the two structural tendencies mentioned above.

A truly multicultural education will be one that can address simultaneously the requirements of global and national integration, and the specific needs of particular culturally distinct communities, both in rural and urban settings. It will lead to an awareness of diversity and to respect for others, whether those others are my nextdoor neighbours, workers in the field, or my fellow human beings in a faraway country. To achieve such a truly pluralistic education it will be necessary to rethink the objectives of what it means to educate and be educated; to remodel the contents and the curricula of formal schooling institutions; to develop new teaching skills and educational methods; and to stimulate the emergence of new generations of teachers/learners.

A truly pluralistic education is based on a philosophy of humanistic pluralism. This is an ethos that prizes the social realities of cultural pluralism. The values of humanistic and cultural pluralism that are necessary to inspire such educational transformation are sometimes lacking; they must be generated in the educational process itself and will in turn be strengthened by it. Many observers, however, have serious doubts about cultural pluralism and its expression in multicultural education. While paying lip service to cultural diversity, they nevertheless question the wisdom of furthering diversity through education. They fear that this may lead to the crystallisation of separate identities, the strengthening of ethnocentrism, the proliferation of ethnic animosities and, finally, to the disintegration of existing nation-states.

There are certainly many current examples of exaggerated ethnic nationalisms leading to political separatism and societal breakdown, not to mention genocidal massacres and hate-filled ethnic cleansings. Yet ethnic diversity cannot be wished away and it is unrealistic to blame multiculturalist policies for the numerous conflicts that in many instances arise precisely because ethnic diversity goes unrecognised or is suppressed.

The criticism of multiculturalism may come from ethnic nationalists who feel that the 'essence' of their nation is being undermined by foreign elements. But it may also come from concerned liberals who want to build the 'civic' nation in which every single individual has the same worth as any other, regardless of race, language, nationality, religion or culture. They feel that by emphasising cultural or ethnic distinctions, borders and walls are erected between otherwise equal – if not always identical – human beings. It is only through education tending toward a truly civic culture to be shared by all that differences will cease to beget inequalities and distinctiveness will no longer generate enmity. In such a worldview, ethnic identities will belong to the purely private domain, and should be of no concern to public policies. While that is surely a worthy vision, we see all around us that ethnic groups do mobilise around cultural symbols and beliefs, and that education systems are in fact at stake in today's 'cultural wars'. Whether such struggles are deeply embedded in the collective psyche or are simply manipulated by opportunistic 'ethnic entrepreneurs', it is not by relegating them to the backroom that democratic, humanistic values can be fostered.

EDUCATION AS A TOOL OF INTEGRATION

The efficiency of formal education as an instrument of integration and social cohesion is thus being increasingly called into question as rapid structural changes associated with the multiple processes of globalisation weaken traditional models of social, political and economic organisation. Concerns with the deterioration of social cohesion are most often related to observed increases in inequalities in income distribution both within and across countries, increases in social exclusion and an apparent rise in the incidence of diverse manifestations of violence in all societies.

Social exclusion, armed conflict, and school-based violence have recently emerged as important social concerns calling for a radical re-examination of the role of education in ensuring social cohesion. In attempting to establish links between processes of social exclusion and violence, it is crucial to bear in mind that exclusion from basic social services, modes of production, security, political participation, or from citizenship, is first and foremost a clear violation of basic human rights. Attempts at establishing links between processes of social exclusion and diverse manifestations of violence must not cloud the fact that the main issue is not simply a functional concern with violence reduction and the strengthening of social cohesion.

Any attempt at identifying and exploring the interrelations between social exclusion, violence and education requires clear definitions of the boundaries of these normative terms. Although widely used, terms such as violence and social exclusion contain multiple components and may be approached in different ways. As a result, they are difficult to define and a differential focus on any of the constituent components produces very different interpretations and usages of the concept. The absence of a clear UNESCO and accurate definition of what is meant by the terms undermines their analytical relevance.

The term social exclusion is a social paradigm originating in Western Europe at least some 40 years ago and used in reference to exclusion of the poor from the benefits associated with economic growth and progress. At that time, the term described a state of poverty and vulnerability, of social inadaptation and marginalisation. The progressive association of the notion of exclusion with equality has made the term analytically relevant for policy formulation through the focus on the identification, not only of groups defined as excluded, but more importantly, on the political and cultural processes that generate inequality and exclusion. Within this framework, both the process and content of formal education; that is, the indadptation and uniformity of schooling, combined with inequalities in access, were seen as contributing to the reproduction of wider social inequalities and exclusion.

As of the mid-seventies, the term social exclusion became used essentially in reference to the emergence of structural unemployment. It designated not only exclusion from the labour market, but also from the accompanying socialisation experienced through access to consumption, identity and the social recognition associated with income generating activity. Exclusion from the labour market thus denoted a risk of marginalisation—a weakening, or even a breakdown, of social bonds associated with integration in the labour market.

Inequalities in access to employment, income, and consumption, social exclusion came to be associated with processes of accumulation of social handicaps and the progressive breakdown of social bonds. Since the initial static definition in terms of poverty lines, social exclusion has since taken on a more dynamic and multidimensional connotation. More than a simple description of a state, social exclusion now attempts to capture the various political, social and economic processes of social disadvantage that produce a state of exclusion. The notion may therefore be seen as encompassing a series of exclusions that may be economic in nature, political, or social.

Although such forms of exclusion are first and foremost a violation of basic human rights, the resulting weakening or breakdown of social bonds, or what may be termed "de-socialisation" or "social disintegration", at the familial, economic, symbolic, political or cultural levels, may be perceived as weakening social cohesion and potentially contributing to social instability and violence.

The current expansion of the application of the term violence often obscures fundamental distinctions between the nature and level of violence and reduces the analytical relevance of the term. Indeed, a single, broad sweeping definition of violence covering a wide array of human interactions ranging, for example, from the collective violence of armed conflict, to individual acts of agression in the street or in the home, to forms of denial of human dignity associated with extreme poverty, is of questionable utility for social analysis. A crucial distinction therefore needs to be made between overt visible forms of (active) violence related to individual acts of physical violence, to gang violence and armed conflict, for instance, and covert invisible (passive) forms of structural, symbolic and cultural violence.

Armed conflict is the most extreme manifestation of collective violence and educational systems are among its many victims. Indeed, intentional and unintentional destruction of physical infrastructure, killing and enlistment of students and teachers, widespread insecurity, curfews, collapsing management structures and dwindling resources constitute important impediments to fulfilling the right to basic education in conflict affected areas.

During the past decade of international efforts toward EFA, political violence was progressively recognised as an "emerging challenge" and the "needs of children and adults affected by armed conflict" came to figure in the Dakar Framework for Action. Although not new, the phenomenon of school-based violence points to a social problem of increasing importance in countries both in the North and South as is reflected in the increasing media coverage of this complex phenomenon. Physical and symbolic manifestations of school-based violence are multiple and include bullying between youngsters, intimidation and physical agression towards teaching personnel, vandalism, racketeering, and sexual violence.

The symbolic and cultural violence of schooling largely reproduce and perpetuate structural inequalities. Learners from minority, immigrant, and other possibly disadvantaged groups are often less-well equipped to adjust to the normative and social demands of school culture that is anchored in middle class values. Anti-school violence may be interpreted as a response to the violence of the educational process itself and to the inability of schooling to adapt to changes in the wider social environment. School-based violence may also be a reflection of violence in wider society, as active or passive participation of youth in domestic, street and political violence has direct repercussions on their learning experience in school.

As both an instrument of domination and oppression, or of democracy and liberation, education can incite conflict and violence. The growing recognition that education is often a target of political violence has prompted a greater concern with the ways in which the content and process of education may actually contribute to precipitate the outbreak and development of violent conflict. The Dakar thematic assessment study on education in emergencies recognised that "weaknesses in education structures and content may have contributed to civil conflict" and that "an education system that reinforces social fissures can represent a dangerous source of conflict".

Although the concept of social exclusion clearly overlaps with more conventional conceptual frameworks such as poverty, inequality, and marginalisation, educational exclusion is often seen as being central to other processes of exclusion. The continued denial of access to basic education for a significant proportion of children in many regions of the world dramatically demonstrates how formal education systems contribute to perpetuating economic disparities and inequalities. The recent shift in focus from supply to demand-side considerations when approaching the issue of educational exclusion, indicates that household poverty and the quality of educational provision have become key to understanding why over 110 million primary school-age children in the developing world continue to be denied access to school.

Exclusion from education may be seen as "part of an intricate web of human rights violations", and the widespread and increasing failure of schooling to ensure socio-economic integration of individuals and groups to the labour market, to adequate levels of consumption, for example, questions the efficiency of formal education as an instrument both of redistribution and of upward mobility. Formal education may therefore contribute to income disparities and social exclusion.

The differential identities that result from a structure of inequality may constitute an important threat to social cohesion and to a common sense of national identity. Furthermore, the failure of formal education in its nation-building and distributive functions is often accompanied by the creation of false expectations and frustrations among those who are economically, culturally and politically excluded, thereby undermining the legitimacy of existing power structures and exacerbating existing social tensions and conflicts and the potential for violence.

In its most general acceptation, education may be defined as the combined processes of socialisation that results in the reproduction of knowledge, norms, values, beliefs and myths from one generation to another. The schooling system is the historically dominant institutional model of formal education and a central instrument of social cohesion. In its central function of nation-building, schooling destroys traditional social bonds of the extended family, the clan or group and institutes a direct relationship between individuals as citizens and the state at national level. In doing so, tensions and conflicts are often generated between local culture and national culture imposed through schooling.

Moreover, the increasing competition and contradiction between the values, attitudes, beliefs and world views transmitted by diverse agents of socialisation such as the family, peer groups, schooling, the media, and religious organisations, erode traditional sources of normative authority and constitute an additional threat to social cohesion, particularly in a context of deteriorating relevance of the nation-state model of organisation in the lives of individuals and communities.

Schooling functions as an ideological vehicle for political domination. This can be explicitly achieved through authoritarian educational structures functioning as mediums of repression, apartheid and discrimination, or through symbolic forms of violence such as the imposition of an official language of instruction in a multilingual context. Political socialisation is also shaped by what is transmitted through the official curriculum, particularly in such subject areas as civic education, history, geography and religious studies. In recognition of that fact, there has been a greater recent emphasis in educational research on content analysis of textbooks in terms of their portrayal of in and out group identity and their potential indirect contribution to conflict and communal strife.

More generally, schooling systems may also fail in their function of political socialisation creating often unintended consequences in terms of greater awareness of educational and social processes generating inequality, discrimination and domination. In the absence of possibilities for greater political representation and participation, violence may constitute the sole mode of conflict resolution.

While the content and unintended consequences of schooling may act as precipitating factors in the general breakdown of social cohesion and the possible outbreak of violence and armed conflict, formal education has an important role to play in strengthening or rebuilding social cohesion in the wake of violent conflict.

In the case of school-based violence, measures taken to prevent or reduce the incidence of violence are commonly articulated around information, prevention, and repression. In addition to the necessary external controls of repressive measures, preventing violence aims to develop a commitment to norms and values imbedded in social networks may inhibit the recourse to violent behaviour.

A wide range of educational initiatives aiming at promoting tolerance, mutual understanding, and nonviolence, often grouped under the heading of peace education all potentially contribute to strengthening or rebuilding social cohesion. Peace education initiatives, however, are often based on a number of underlying assumptions that are not always properly supported by evidence. Peace education initiatives often tend to focus on the level of interpersonal behaviour, while so much of violent conflict is generated at the group level.

FOSTERING UNIVERSAL VALUES

While striving for preservation of cultural identity and traditions, nations have been increasingly aware of interregional interdependence. In response to increasing globalisation, there have been advocacy efforts made by multicultural education systems to facilitate a desirable core of universal values, which have included the following:

— *Awareness of human rights combined with a sense of social responsibilities*. Caution is taken that rights are not separated from duties, that the concept of human rights is not imposed from a western ethnocentric perspective but related to cultural traditions and national/regional contexts, and that the rights of individuals are linked to those of the collectives.

— Value of social equity and democratic participation in decision-making and government, which will be the 'central objective in all parts of life'.

— Understanding and tolerance of cultural differences and pluralism, which is a precondition of social cohesion, peaceful co-existence and conflict-resolution by negotiation instead of force, and ultimately of world peace.

— *A spirit of caring,* a 'keynote value for future education', and an intrinsic quality of human compassion, which should be extended not only to the family members and colleagues, but to all the disadvantaged, the sick, the poor and the disabled, for the well-being of humankind and our planet.

— *Cooperative spirit,* while competition can be observed in all spheres of daily life, cooperation is all the more necessary.

— *Enterprising spirit,* a quality which is needed not only for economic productivity and competitiveness but for all life situations.

— *Creativity,* which will always be needed for technological advances, social progress, economic dynamics and all other human endeavours.

— *Sensitivity to gender equality,* which has been recognised as 'the key to development and poverty alleviation',and 'both a gateway to development and a measure of that development'.

— *Open-mindedness to change,* which will be the only thing which will not change, and the attitude not only to accept change but to act as an agent of positive change.

— Sense of obligation to environment protection and sustainable development, so as not to create economic, social and ecological debts for future generations.

Most of these universal values needed for the twenty-first century have long been embedded in the age-old cultural traditions of human civilisations. They encompass the moral visions and ideals of truth, kindness, beauty, justice and liberty which were elaborated long ago by our predecessors and magnificently preserved in the treasuries of thought.

Altruism, originating in the love of one human being for another, has been respected as the highest human value for hundreds of years. One way to foster universal values for future centuries is to educate the young with great books of the past and inherit the fine traditions of humanity. Another approach to the cultivation of these universal values for global ethics is to promote, by means of education, cross-cultural learning between Eastern and Western cultures.

Culturally the East and West are compatible and complementary rather than contradictory and mutually opposing. The Confucian aristocracy ('scholar-official') of merit, rather than hereditary privilege, was closest to the ancient Greek idea of 'government by the best'. The East's cultural learning from the west has evolved from the material dimension (modern technologies) to the institutional (political infrastructure) and the socio-psychological (values and beliefs) dimensions. It is multicultral education that has provided bridges between eastern and western cultures.

If and when the East and West could learn and benefit from each other, integrating each other's cultural strengths, for example, the individual initiative with the collective team spirit, competitiveness with cooperativeness, the technological capacities with the moral qualities – then desirable universal values will gradually develop and a global ethic will be formed, which will be a fundamental renewal of cultures and a great contribution of multicultural education to humanity.

References

Banks, J.A., *An Introduction to Multicultual Education,* Boston Mass, Allyn and Bacon 1999.

Burnett, G., *Varieties of Multicultural Education*, New York, ERIC clearinghouse on Urban Education 1998

Delpit, Lisa, "The Silenced Dialogue: Power and Pedagogy in Educating Other People's Children", *Harvard Education Review*, 58, (3) (1988), 280-298.

Friedman, J., *Cultural Identity and Global Process*, Sage, London, 1994.

Knight, J., "Internationalisation of higher education: a conceptual framework", in Knight, J. De Wit, H. (eds.), *Internationalisation of Higher Education in Asia Pacific Countries*, European Association for International Education, Amsterdam, 1997.

Margo Okazama-Rey (ed)., *Beyond Heroes and Holidays*, Washington, D.C.: Network of Educators on the Americas, 1997.

Sleeter, Christine and Grant, *Making Choices for Multicultural Education: Five approaches to race, class, and gender*, New York: Merrill, 1994.

Yang, R., "University internationalisation: its meanings, rationales and implications", *International Education*, Vol.13, No 1, 2002.

9

Challenges of Multicultural Education

Nowadays the concept of internationalisation is popular and frequently used, in varying context and for diverse purposes. Yet it remains ambiguous and unclear. The English writer J. Bentham, was the first to use the term "international" around 1780. Etymologically it can be derived from Latin; "inter" means "between" and "nationalisation" refers to "nation". Hence, the concept of internationalisation applies to, on the one hand, a process of "making something international". It is a process of exchange and mutual influence, where the actors involved are presumably "nations".

Intercultural education implies a learning situation characterised by intercultural interaction, which is used actively as a pedagogic resource. Since "cultures" or "ethnicities" rather than "nations" are the centre of attention in this text, the term internationalisation, therefore, will be substituted for intercultural education when it seems more adequate.

Internationalisation is habitually seen as something unique for the last two centuries. But ever since time immemorial, people have interacted with other cultures, out of curiosity, necessity or by sheer coincidence. Explorers such as James Cook, Vasco da Gama, Christopher Columbus, travelled the world in their thirst for knowledge and impulses. Famous Swedish scientists Carl von Linne and Emanuel Swedenborg worked in different parts of the world. Academics and students travelled abroad to the universities in Bologna, Göttingen, Paris, Greifsvald, Oxford, to mention just a few, to take advantage of the intellectual elite of those days. Thus, interest in the world, other people, cultures, languages and ideas or simply the quest for knowledge and competence have always been motives for academic training abroad. A major difference is, however, that nowadays we live in a globalised world. People, capital, ideologies, media images and cultural impulses travel around the world more rapidly and efficiently than ever before.

International experiences are constantly available for many of us in our own neighbourhoods. The internet connects people of different backgrounds across large distances. But the unique thing is that the internet is totally indifferent to international boundaries. It links together people who otherwise would be strangers to one another, by a common interest that has nothing to do with nationality.

"Virtual reality" has become a significant factor in many people's identity construction Against this background, "territorial" identities have presumably been substituted for "mobile" identities. Overall, in the late modern world identities are more fragile, dispersed or dislocated and have urged the construction of new identities.

Responding to the needs of global man, education policies have become increasingly internationalised. A clear tendency toward an ideologisation of internationalisation policies is also visible. Policymakers and educators, frequently and energetically, stress internationalisation as a principal goal for education.

Internationalisation ideologies can be seen as integral elements of an "identity-project" to replace territorial, communal and national identities with mobile, cosmopolitan and "international" identities. For single individuals, it may be simultaneously an answer to their personal quest for an identity. Furthermore, internationalisation is no longer, however, a concern exclusively for universities, colleges or research institutes.

For a variety of reasons, multinational organisations, companies or political bodies also define their internationalisation policies. Consequently, there is a viable discourse on internationalisation. Policymakers tend to focus on ideological goals, university administrators on formalities and practicalities of international cooperation whereas teachers emphasise pedagogic issues. In addition to this, universities struggle to overcome organisational obstacles, traditions and collective attitudes that prevent administrators and teaching staff from cooperating sufficiently and adequately.

The internationalisation of education can contribute to a more democratic, fair and equal world. It increases the awareness of the varying life-conditions, social injustices and racial segregation that people live under. Over time this may initiate a redistribution of resources and welfare. The rationale of international cooperation in academia seems grounded in a commonsense assumption that internationalisation is good *per se.*

International cooperation grants presumably students and staff from the "poor world" access to new knowledge and competence. But it should also, to the students, communicate and create understanding for the relativity of cultural beliefs, values, living patterns, ideologies and ideas. It should, among them, inoculate tolerance, respect and contribute to a sense of global as well as national community and solidarity and work against ethnocentrism, racism and academic self-righteousness. The aim should be to evoke students' curiosity and stimulate their appreciation of intercultural differences and ethnic diversity.

Higher education has become a global commodity and countries market themselves as research and education nations. Critics claim that the wealthy nations, through international exchange programmes try to attract researchers, teaching staff and fee-paying students from the "poor world" in order to keep their competence in the country, thus risking to "brain drain" their home countries.

Critics claim also that internationalisation is guided by the "rich world's" economic and political interests, standards, value systems, ethnocentrism and belief in self-superiority. Hence, internationalisation is predominantly seen as a one-way flow—"they" can learn from us, but "we" have little to learn from them. In its most extreme guise, they mean that internationalisation is an instrument to "educate uncivilised people" or simply a strategy to maximise profit and ensure economic growth.

For the European Union the implementation of international cooperation is part of a large-scale identity project. Internationalisation-policies are considered potent means to strengthen a sense of community and association among the Union's members. To simplify student mobility actions have been taken to increase transparency, equivalence and recognition. Similarly, many countries initiate international programmes for their citizens. Sweden and the European Union have allocated vast resources to increase the level of student exchanges and international research cooperation.

Intercultural education is assumed to match demands of the global and multicultural world. It may be a way to enhance the labour force's professional and intercultural competencies , but also to better take advantage of the inherent potential of domestic ethnic diversity. Many employers stress and vaule the need for professionals with competencies in several languages and knowledge of diverse cultural codes. Motives may be to maximise profit, expand into new markets or increase efficiency. For this reason, international experiences constitute a comparative advantage for students as they later seek employment.

Traditionally, ideologies and policies on domestic ethnic and cultural pluralism have been separated from those on internationalisation. Questions of internationalisation and domestic ethnic diversity are, however, two sides of the same coin. It would, therefore, be more fruitful and productive to work with these matters in an integrated fashion.

Domestic "immigrant" students have much to contribute with in discussions on international or intercultural issues as well as to any other issues for that matter. By integrating them in international courses and programmes higher education is not only international but rather intercultural in its scope, ambitions and theoretical analyses. Moreover, this ensures intercultural education for students who, for different reasons, cannot study abroad.

Whereas internationalisation policies typically emphasise the beneficial opportunity of studying abroad, policies on ethnic diversity merely talk of equal opportunity. Whereas internationalisation is said to enrich education, programmes on ethnic diversity merely want to make them available or easier. And, whereas internationalisation-policies stress the acquisition of new competencies, ethnic diversity policies aim at taking advantage of already existing competencies among its citizens. By making use of domestic ethnic diversity, intercultural experiences are available for students who cannot go abroad.

Intercultural education may be the answer to the competence needs of the future. Intercultural education — at home or abroad — can be viewed as a journey. More specifically, it is four parallel but closely interconnected journeys. It is an academic journey where the student is exposed and must adapt to a different academic setting, with its own unique culture, teaching style, interaction patterns, social norms, grading system etc.

By being abroad the features and oddities of the home institution tend to crystallise. Similarly, students may become aware of the cultural bias in education. They can, for instance, be given assignments where they are asked to scrutinise syllabi and contents of lectures and literature to see how they are culturally biased.

Intercultural education also constitutes a cultural journey where students are confronted with a new, perhaps unknown, national culture — with its unique features, language and so on. Again, this process brings about cross-cultural comparisons, where the host culture's unique features are in focus, but also illuminates the home culture's peculiarities.

It is an intellectual journey where the students hopefully become aware of their frame of reference and critically reflect over their attitudes, prejudices, stereotypes and ethnocentrism. They should be urged to challenge their taken-for-granted conceptions and be assisted, not merely in detecting cultural differences and similarities but in understanding and respecting them. Moreover, intercultural education should stimulate students to move beyond instrumental learning. Instead they should be encouraged to reflect over the process of learning and adopt "an outsider's perspective".

Finally, it constitutes an emotional journey since it is likely to bring about a vast array of emotional responses. Being a stranger, newcomer, alien or simply finding oneself in an unfamiliar or intercultural setting may trigger feelings of uncertainty, uneasiness, frustration, anxiety or chauvinism. International education can make them aware of emotional processes and, in turn, help them to develop fruitful coping strategies for the future. For the individual, intercultural education may contribute to personal growth and self-actualisation as well as to his or her life quality and sense of identity.

Pedagogic Challenges

Intercultural student groups pose certain pedagogic challenges. Typically international students demand *fingerspitzengefühl*, as well as more effort and commitment. Teachers are likely to become more involved in the life-process of the students than in other students. They turn to you with grievances — not merely academic but also personal problems. Thus, to a higher extent the teacher role is entangled with the mentor and counsellor roles.

A particular challenge for the staff is teaching in foreign language. For some this is an unbridgeable gulf, whereas it only demands a short period of adjustment for others. Nonetheless, to many of us it may be constraining, when it comes to exemplifying or explaining something. To facilitate intercultural education, language training at a variety of competence levels should be available to students and staff.

In addition to qualitative gains, there must be other incentives for teaching-staff, who take on intercultural classes. Large financial and personnel resources and time may have to be allocated — for the course as such but also for assessment, modifications of the pedagogic design, student interaction, workshops, guest-speakers, etc. More than other courses, in international courses the structure, expectations on students, grading system must be transparent. As an expression of professionalism or to avoid problems or misunderstandings, some teachers inform students about everything that they are likely to experience in the new setting. But providing too much apriori knowledge may devalue the students' experiences.

Courses that, at first sight, seem to lack an intercultural dimension most often embody intercultural components. An innovative teacher can discover such dimensions in almost any course. For example, by discussing "science" as a cultural construction students may see the relativity of the most fundamental "principles" of science, e.g., logic, induction, deduction, production of knowledge and disciplinary boundaries. Or by directing attention to controversial themes, values, norms, habits, customs traditions, etc, international education can bring attention to cultural peculiarities and similarities.

Staff-student and student-student interaction and by approaching topics from different angles, ideological and theoretical perspectives may produce synergy effects. To optimise the learning experience the teacher must serve as a facilitator, guiding the processes of self-reflection. International guest speakers may also have positive effects on the overall quality of the class — simply because he or she has an area of interest or teaching style that differs from the regular teacher's. Important is, however, that students are able to connect the guest speaker's contribution to the course contents. All too often guest speakers are used as sort of an "international choreography" to meet the requirements of students and syllabi.

Educators must be brave enough to allow a certain level of frustration as well as skilled enough to assist students in coping with uncertainty and vagueness, since a classroom atmosphere characterised by constructive frustration facilitates learning. "Trial and error"— or rather "learning by struggling" seems to be useful method. The same goes for the teacher; any problem houses pedagogic possibilities. Identifying and taking advantage of it is, however, the challenge.

At many universities there are traditions, collective attitudes and an organisational dichotomy — administrators and teaching staff — that are counterproductive to these ambitions. Therefore, there is a need for further discussions and analyses of the goals, possibilities and challenges of intercultural education. Administrators and teaching staff must co-operate to a much higher degree than before.

Current conceptions on internationalisation are not only ambiguous, but also far from sufficiently ambitious. All too often form-issues have been the predominant focus of discussions. Besides form-issues, it is time to focus on content issues, e.g., ideological and cultural biases in course literature, perspectives and scientific assumptions — and on pedagogic considerations, e.g., the inherent learning potential and possible pedagogic problems of intercultural study groups.

Issues of Global and Local diversity

Local diversity was the main reason for the development of multicultural education. From the beginning, multicultural education laid great emphasis on culture and mutual cultural exchange. In the beginnings of multicultural education, relativism of cultures was taken for granted whereas the current view is that the reflection on cultures is more complex. There are two implications to be found in the importance of culture:

i) Mutual learning about cultures requires an awareness of cultural differences in all questions, which supports a division into the own and the other — an important point in the multicultural education discourse;

ii) The focus on culture also made it easier to include global aspects, e.g., cultures of different nations and people.

The focus on culture has been criticised by educationalists but the name 'intercultural'/ 'multicultural' is too strong, so that, for example, students in general define multicultural education as 'dealing with foreign cultures', which includes the cultures of migrant students, since their cultures are regarded as foreign as well. Therefore, one of the challenges multicultural education has to face is to overcome the focus on culture and instead to deal with individual diversity.

This concept focused on racism, discrimination and inequality — barriers that have to be overcome before mutual exchange is possible. Multicultural education with a focus on local diversity has helped to open schools, curricula and schoolbooks for diversity due to migration. While multicultural education had only reluctantly been accepted into the educational administration, the word now became quickly accepted.

Multicultural education supports bilingual education of migrant students, though mainly in an uncoordinated way. Bilingual classes in the proper sense would make it necessary to separate migrant students and offer them instruction in linguistically homogeneous classes, which is a contradiction to the ideal of integration. There are very few exceptions, like the concept of bilingual literacy courses where migrant students attend regular classes but learn to read and write parallel in both languages with the help of coordinated teamwork between the classroom teacher and the mother tongue teacher;

'Multicultural learning' has become a goal in all language classes and foreign language didactics deal with multicultural learning. Intercultural communication has always had a strong relationship to international communication since it was originally examined mainly with regard to business communication.

Educational research within multicultural education also has to meet the fact that not all immigration is permanent, because there is an increasing trend towards transmigration processes. Permanent migration has been understood as a more or less unidirectional movement from one nation-state to another, including the possibility of remigration as a second step that can be regarded as a unidirectional movement as well since it is also a permanent process.

Now we face different forms of migration in the late twentieth and beginning twenty-first century where globalisation plays a key role. Transmigration is understood as a specific type of migration in transnational social spaces. It is shown that migrants develop multidirectional patterns of migration with different social and spatial relations. These patterns may differ between groups as well as between individuals. These shifts in social reality challenge the framework for analysis in social science as well as in educational theory and practice, though the group of asylum seekers and refugees has always been regarded as non-permanent migrants, so that multicultural education could not completely focus on multiculturalism as a permanency.

The main challenges in education that result from new forms of migration are:

i) So far, language education focuses far more on fluency than on bilingualism.

ii) So far, schools have nearly no concepts for students who enter school in the course of a school year, but this can easily happen in families with high mobility;

iii) So far, multicultural education has a strong focus on social education — this can be explained by the fact that work and refugee migrants were so far mainly underprivileged and marginalised. Transnational migrants are often persons with a high qualification and a good social standing.

iv) So far, integration is the keyword in political as well as in educational discussions on migration. It has to be questioned whether the model of integration in the concept of multiculturalism is compatible with transmigration where migrants live in more than one social and spatial context, either at the same time, in consecutive periods or in a way where social and geographical spaces are split or overlap.

The challenges of transnational migration have only recently been considered and are still not in the center of multicultural education. It would certainly not be appropriate to put transnational migration into the middle of multicultural education, but it has to be considered, especially in the sense that these different forms of migration — and thus migrant students — will all be together in classes, so that a broad range of concepts have to be put together to find a suitable education for all students.

Challenges of Digital Divide

'Digital divide' is a term used to denote inequalities in access to computers and the internet between groups of people based on one or more social or cultural identifiers. Under this conceptualisation, researchers tend to compare rates of access to these technologies across individuals or schools based on race, sex, disability status, and other identity dimensions. The term 'divide' refers to the difference in access rates among groups. The racial digital divide, for example, describes the difference in rates of access to computers and the internet, at home and school, between those racial groups with high rates of access and those with lower rates of access.

Similarly, the sex- or gender digital divide refers to the gap in access rates between men and women. By the end of 2000, when women surpassed men to become a majority of the United States online population, many people also believed the sex digital divide had disappeared. If there were more women than men using the internet, the logic went, equality had been achieved. Girls and women were equally likely to use computers and the internet as boys and men. Still, though the fact that more girls and women were using the internet is a meaningful step forward, a broader and deeper look at their position in relation to the increasingly techno-centric society and global economy, reveals that equality in access is considerably different from equity in opportunity.

Most of the sex and gender inequities in society and other media are replicated online. The ever-present and ever-growing internet pornography industry, along with the threat of cyber-stalking and the relative ease with which potential sexual predators can attain personal information about women online, make the internet a hostile—and potentially dangerous—environment for many girls and women. Equally hostile to women are academic and professional pursuits of mathematics, sciences, engineering, computer sciences—all traditionally male fields that are closely linked with computers and the internet.

Research shows how women and girls are systematically steered away from these fields beginning as early as elementary school through school culture, classroom climate, traditional gender roles, and other societal pressures. Additionally, video games, largely marketed for men and boys, often depict girls and women as damsels in distress or sideshow prostitutes. Most video game makers are men and most video game consumers are boys and men. So, instead of critiquing this fact and considering why it is so, the producers bow to market pressures and recycle the industry sexism.

In fact, the glaring inequities that remain despite equality in internet access illustrate the urgency for a deeper, broader understanding of the digital divide and a deeper, broader approach for eliminating it. These remaining inequities, which mirror deeply entrenched and historically cycled inequities in professional, economic, and education opportunities for women, together serve as a clear, powerful critique of the unidimensional approach most often employed for addressing the race and class digital divides: simply providing schools and communities with more computers and more, or faster, internet access. Though this is a positive step forward, it fails to address social, cultural, and political factors that will be in place with or without more machinery.

The traditional understanding of the digital divide as gaps in rates of physical access to computers and the internet fails to capture the full picture of the divide, its stronghold, and its educational, social, cultural, and economic ramifications. Meanwhile, such a narrow conceptualisation of the divide serves the interests of privileged groups who can continue to critique access rates instead of thinking critically and reflectively about their personal and collective roles in cycling and recycling old inequities in a new cyber-form. A new understanding of the digital divide is needed, one that provides adequate context and begins with a dedication to equity and social justice throughout education. Multicultural education—a field that enters every discussion about education with this dedication—offers an important, desperately needed framework for such an understanding.

In his book *Understanding the Digital Divide from a Multicultural Education Framework,* Paul Gorski crafted the following statement about understanding and eliminating the digital divide.

"A multicultural education approach to understanding and eliminating the digital divide:

— critiques technology-related inequities in the context of larger educational and societal inequities, keeping at the fore of the discussion the fact that those groups most disenfranchised by the digital divide are the same groups historically disenfranchised by curricular and pedagogical practices, evaluation and assessment, school counselling, and all other aspects of education;

— broadens the significance of "access" beyond that of physical access to computers and the internet to include access to support and encouragement to pursue and value technology-related fields, educationally and professionally;

— broadens the significance of "access" beyond that of physical access to computers and the internet to include access to non-hostile, inclusive software and internet content;

— critically examines not only who has access to computers and the internet, but how these technologies are being used by various people or identity groups or by those teaching various people or groups;

— considers, in the context of studying access rates with this broader definition of "access," the larger socio-political ramifications of, and socio-economic motivations for, the expanding significance of information technology, not only in schools, but in society at large, and how the growing merger of cyber-culture with wider culture privileges those who already have access in the broadest sense;

— confronts capitalistic propaganda, like commercials portraying children from around the world announcing their recent arrival online, that lead people to believe that these technologies are available to everyone, everywhere, under any conditions, who want to use them;

— rejects as simplistic and patriarchal any programme that purports to "close" the divide only by providing more computers and more, or faster, internet access, to a school, library, or other public place;

— rejects as inadequate any solution that aims to "close" and not "eliminate" the divide; and

— conceptualises the elimination of the digital divide as those actions that:

  — lead to, and maintain, a present and future in which all people, regardless of race, ethnicity, sex, gender, sexual orientation, socio-economic class, disability status, age, education level, or any other social or cultural identity, enjoy equitable access—safe, comfortable, encouraged and encouraging, non-hostile, and valued physical, cultural, social access—to information technology including software, computers, the and internet;

  — lead to, and maintain, a present and future in which all people, regardless of race, ethnicity, sex, gender, sexual orientation, socio-economic class, disability status, age, education level, or any other social or cultural identity, enjoy equitable access—safe, comfortable, encouraged and encouraging, non-hostile, and valued physical, cultural, social access—to educational pursuits in technology-related fields including mathematics, science, computer science, and engineering;

— lead to, and maintain, a present and future in which all people, regardless of race, ethnicity, sex, gender, sexual orientation, socioeconomic class, disability status, age, education level, or any other social or cultural identity, enjoy equitable access—safe, comfortable, encouraged and encouraging, non-hostile, and valued physical, cultural, social access—to career pursuits in technology-related fields including mathematics, science, computer science, engineering, and information technology;

— lead to, and maintain, a present and future in which all people, regardless of race, ethnicity, sex, gender, sexual orientation, socioeconomic class, disability status, age, education level, or any other social or cultural identity, play an equitable role in determining the socio-cultural significance of computers and the internet and the overall social and cultural value of these technologies; and

— lead to, and maintain, a present and future in which all of these conditions are constantly monitored, examined, and ensured through a variety of perspectives and frameworks.

As new technologies become more and more interwoven with all aspects of life and well-being, it becomes equally urgent to employ the complexities and critiques of multicultural education theory and practice to the problem of the digital divide. It is the next—the present—equity issue in schools and larger society with enormous social justice implications. This re-framing of the digital divide can serve as a starting point for more active participation in digital divide research and action within the field of multicultural education.

References

Extra Guus, Yagmur Kutlay, *Language diversity in multicultural Europe*, Paris: UNESCO, 2002.

Hinnenkamp, Volker, "Constructing Misunderstanding as a Cultural Event" In: A. di Luzio, S. Günthner & F. Orletti (eds.), *Culture in Communication. Analyses of intercultural situations*, Amsterdam / Philadelphia: J. Benjamins, 2001.

Hoff, Gerd, "Multicultural Education in Germany: Historical Development and Current Status", In J. A. Banks & C. A. M. Banks (eds.), *Handbook of Research on Multicultural Education*, New York: MacMillan, 1995.

Luchtenberg, Sigrid (ed.), *Migration, Education and Change*, London: Routledge, 2003.

Watts and Jerzy J. Smolicz (eds.), *Cultural Democracy and Ethnic Pluralism, Multicultural and multilingual Policies in Education*, Bern et al.: Peter Lang Verlag, 125-148, 1997.

10

Racial, Ethnic, Gender and Class Issues

The growing globalisation on an economic scale brings changes in all spheres of human life, personally, socially, culturally. The significance of time and space vanishes. Increasing communication technology brings us closer together, lets our knowledge grow. Individual responsibility seems to grow and disappear at once. The gap between rich and poor grows, but the effects on each other are less visible. Nowadays, people from different cultural backgrounds often live together in one society. More information and mobility on the one hand, unjust political and economic circumstances on the other contribute to migration flows between many countries. The world seems to develop in a closely interrelated way, celebrating common cultural events, such as the World Olympics.

The new pluralist and multicultural societies also give rise to uncertainty. Traditional cultural reference points vanish; the increasing diversity can be perceived as a threat to what we call our identity. Main elements and references are rapidly changing or losing meaning: nation, territory, religious belonging, political ideology, profession, family. Traditional patterns of belonging break up and come together to form new expressions of culture. So, we are again like "nomads" searching for new references, more and more individually based. Ideologically closed groups such as sects grow, nationalism is revived, responsibility shifted to "strong leaders". Economic uncertainty, growing social injustice and polarisation contribute to insecurity. A global understanding with unclear consequences often competes with the interest of belonging to a particular, clearly defined group.

In a diverse world, where we insist on our differences, the question of power plays a large role. It matters if we belong to the stronger or the weaker part, if our cultural patterns are of a majority or minority. In line with this, new conflicts arise or old ones break out again, religious or ethnic belonging become fearful reasons for war and violence, between as well as within countries and regions. The "clash of civilisations", the "war of cultures" have been announced. Much hurt has been caused in the past, human rights are being permanently violated, because diversity on an equal basis has not been respected, because the majorities have always used their power over minorities.

The discontinuity between the cultures of poor and ethnic minority students and the culture of schooling affects academic underachievement and failure. Moreover, caught in the ambivalence of success and failure in schools that transmit a culture of domination the learning of children of colour and poor children is further hindered by the factors of invisibility, alienation, and resistance.

Much of the overt and covert conflict about race, ethnicity, social class, and gender has been based in the mythology of a superior culture into which all others must be assimilated. The imbalance of power between the dominant culture and subjugated cultures has created centuries of aggression, antagonism, and resistance. Fortunately, the concept that cultural differences enrich, rather than diminish, our society is increasingly acknowledged. It is the suppression of cultures that weakens the society.

The emergence of multicultural education in 1990 aimed to mine the possibilities of plurality through education. It addresses the educational needs of a society that continues to struggle with the realisation that it is not monocultural, but is an amalgamation of many cultures. It harbours a place for a multitude of voices in a multicultural society and a place for many dreams.

Victims of racism and ethnic discrimination and violence worry that attention to other forms of human diversity dilutes multicultural education's ability to address their concerns. Feminists and other proponents of gender equity may feel marginalised within the multicultural education discourse. The complexity of identities that individuals experience makes it difficult to craft a multicultural mission that speaks to the specificity of identity. However, attempts to be all things to all people seem to minimise the effective impact of multicultural education as a vehicle for school and social change.

Multicultural education can be one tool in our efforts to understand the complexity of today's world, by understanding others and ourselves a bit better. Moreover, it can be one of the keys to open the doors into a new society. It may enable us to better face the challenges of current realities. We can understand it as empowerment not just to cope personally with current developments, but to deal with the potential of change, which can have a positive and constructive impact in our societies.

Multicultural education is a personal growing process with collective implications. It always invites us to reflect why we want to deal with it, which visions we have, what we want to achieve through it. Not just taken as a personal acquisition or a luxury for a few people working in an international environment, multicultural education is relevant for how we live together in our societies.

Young people live experiences in general very intensively and are open to all kind of changes. They are often economically and socially dependent and vulnerable to the circumstances they are exposed to. Often, they are the first losers and the first winners in developments. They are the ones to celebrate global culture in blue jeans and with rave parties, they are the ones who have climbed the Berlin Wall first. They study abroad or emigrate, they trespass borders, with valid passports or illegally on adventurous small boats. Consequently, they are most open to multicultural education processes, to get in touch with each other and discover and explore diversity.

But the way many different young people in many different circumstances live does not always provide the appropriate framework for the rich yet difficult processes of multicultural education. When we talk about multicultural education and youth work, we talk about young people dealing with their complex and diverse backgrounds, and this means having to confront things that can appear contradictory.

Some general trends in multicultural education are given below. They show on the one hand the different developments in society that young people have to deal with, and on the other hand how these relate to — and often contradict with — main elements of multicultural education.

— Modern culture emphasises accelerated speed, strong feelings and immediate results, presenting the world rather as a series of intensive events without continuity. This emotional overdose contrasts with the need for rational explanations. Multicultural education is about a constant and slow learning process, full of ruptures. It involves both reason and feelings and their relevance for life.

— Most of the education young people receive favours answers and provides ready concepts, simple patterns of explanation. Media and ads work with simplifications and deepen stereotypes and pre-conceptions. Multicultural education is about diversity and difference, about pluralism, complexity and open questions, finally about reflection and change.

— When youth is addressed as consumer, the satisfaction of individual - mainly materialist - desires is top priority. A very particular type of freedom is promoted: "survival of the fittest". Professional and economic insecurity reinforce competition. Multicultural education is about you and me, about relationships and solidarity and about taking the other seriously.

— Youth finds fewer reference points throughout adolescence; life experiences and the perception of reality are more fragmented. People long for harmony and stability. Multicultural education is about dealing with the forming and alteration of personal identity, about discerning changes of meaning, it is about accepting tensions and contradictions.

— Society gives young people few examples and leaves them few spaces to express and encourage diversity, to insist on the right to be or act differently, to learn about equal chances instead of dominance. Multicultural education is a lot about difference, about diverse life contexts and cultural relativism.

— Youth feels rather powerless as it regards public life. It is difficult to identify political responsibilities and personal participation possibilities in today's complex network of reality. Multicultural education is about democracy and citizenship, it implies taking a stand against oppression, exclusion and their supporting mechanisms.

— Political and public discussions tend to simplify facts, they rarely search for causes. The historic memory transmitted to young people is short and one-sided. Both factors do not prepare young people for a complex reality. Multicultural education is about dealing with memory, remembering and overcoming memories towards a new future.

These trends may look and feel different in different countries and social realities, they are neither complete nor exclusive. Still, they invite us to reflect further on the state of our societies and how multicultural education relates to them, especially in the eyes of young people. Multicultural education processes with young people should be based on their reality. A planned multicultural education situation will have therefore to deal with and integrate contradictory tendencies. When they are discussed openly, they can be potential departure points towards an honest intercultural dialogue.

Strategies to Eliminate Racism from Classroom

The duty and moral obligation of modern educators is to attempt to eliminate racism in today's classrooms. If the role of education truly is to produce a better society, then the teacher must accept the onus of responsibility for this huge undertaking. Educators who practice a reconstructionist philosophy believe it is their duty to be a social activist. They must continually search for means to improve society by ending degradation and harm.

One tactic a teacher could utilise to remove racism from classrooms is to take a critical look at the materials which the students use to learn. Despite the recent trend of multicultural literature, many school texts remain monocultural in their presentation of knowledge. This may send serious messages about the inferiority of some and the superiority of others. Texts that fail to address the issue of multiculturalism by displaying pictures, and using examples, of predominantly white males, may be inadvertently contributing to the problem of racism by promoting stereotypes and prejudices. Teachers should select texts that represent non-mainstream persons positively.

Some believe that the curriculum, through its texts, ought to describe the ways different cultural groups have contributed to western civilisation to eliminate racism. This is apparent in the writings of George Dei when he suggested that information should present truths about the contributions of African societies to world civilisation. This would represent Africans in a more positive light as opposed to consistently dwelling on their problems and failures, which may perpetuate and strengthen existing biases. Texts should also promote equity of people with mental and physical handicaps, the gifted, the elderly and between the genders. The latter may be accomplished by portraying men and women in roles traditionally held by the opposite sex. Students could learn about female doctors, lawyers, and mechanics and concurrently about male secretaries, nurses, and flight attendants.

Cooperative learning groups are not only an effective tool to stimulate academic growth through participation, but they may also be a successful vehicle to help eliminate racism. Through the creation of a team, a micro-society, educators can attempt to break down the superficial barriers that students may see when they are individuals. Group work exposes individual attitudes, ideas, experiences, and beliefs that are used to achieve a common goal through a collective effort. Group work leads to better understanding of the task at hand, the dynamics of team-work, which will be valuable in later stages of life, and opens the lines of communication between group members despite race, sex, age or religion.

Other methods to help eliminate racism may include a variety of active learning strategies through different multi-sensory learning styles. Maria Sweeney's fourth grade class made posters condemning racism, sexism, and ageism. They also watched movies on apartheid and created anti-racist rap songs for a play the students wrote and starred in for the parents to demonstrate the evils of racism. They also encouraged contribution to African relief funds and the joining of anti-racist groups.

Some educators take a Golden Rule approach to eliminating racism. One such popular practice was to expose children to racism and how the sting of discrimination felt by using the blue eye/green eye experiment, which favoured students and gave them preferential treatment based on their eye colour. Multicultural days exploring different cultures, religions, and the history of different races may also occur. Some schools practice a zero-tolerance policy to discourage the practice of racism and other undesirable behaviours, which may result in the removal of the offending student from that particular school.

The methods descibed above have a positive influence on eliminating racism in the classroom. These practices identify racism and suggest how to quell it in schools, but they fail to prepare the student for the racism they will lamentably still encounter in society. Existentialists may find fault with this approach, as the reconstructionists don't seem to address the totality of the situation. Children must learn to accept the fact that racism will exist outside of schools. Existentialists might argue that the educator must focus the evils of racism more on the individual so that each student personally understands racism and it's implications. For if a student cannot relate to racism as it affects himself, then he may not understand it completely and choose not to actively participate in its elimination.

Perhaps Reconstructionists should teach that some people are going to sport racist views no matter what and will not listen to the sappy, humanistic preaching and droning of the anti-racist activist. Students must be taught to accept racists, bigots, sexists, and hate-mongers despite not agreeing with their philosophy or practice, because if they don't accept these people, then they themselves are practicing the prejudice against which they so actively lobby.

Students must learn that racism is an unfortunate part of our society and that attempting to eliminate in schools is a step in the right direction. They must also realise that racism will exist despite their creation of posters and plays and that changing the thought processes and perceptions of certain people cannot be done overnight or even at all.

Multicultural Education and Minorities

Education is one of the most important vehicles by which the integration of minorities into mainstream society can be promoted. Genuine ethnic problems in the education of pupils belonging to minorities manifest themselves in three main areas: language, culture, and discrimination. Beyond that, another major set of problems are raised by failures in the processes of education of the majority in regard to minority issues. In this regard the understanding and valuing of cultural diversity is a key issue.

Minority children frequently have no access to their history, culture and traditions within existing educational programmes. Nor do majority children receive information or knowledge about minority culture. The result is a mutual lack of knowledge, and too often, prejudices in the majority group persist. Discrimination is a problem that all minorities face.

Equal rights and equal opportunities in education for minority pupils in terms of access, treatment and learning outcomes are at the core of that democratic vision. All problems faced by minorities in terms of social positions, human rights, inter ethnic relations and the autonomy of minority groups should be considered. All minority education strategies should be based on a holistic approach, which takes into account all aspects of their "problem world".

A clear distinction should be made between genuine ethnic problems, which are addressed by special school provisions and not ethnic problems, which are addressed by quality education. Non ethnic problems in relation to the education of minorities refer to the quality of the teaching-learning process in general. Children belonging to minorities should have access to the same quality education as their peers belonging to the majority.

Discrimination in education should be prohibited and terminated. However, this doesn't mean only that support of such programmes and schools should be avoided or, where existing, should brought to an end, but also requires active support of reintegration of minority children into the mainstream education. A certain level of separation in education based on the agreement of the parents and the children and on mother tongue or bilingual instruction is not against the overall goal of integration. However, maintaining and supporting separate minority schools should not lead to the "ghettoisation" of the problems of minority and multicultural education. When it is possible, minority and majority children should learn together. In these cases intercultural learning might serve the integration of minority children and the incorporation of minority culture into the content of education, as well.

Children belonging to minorities should have access to their cultural heritage as well as to the culture of the majority. The opportunity to learn about the children's own cultural heritage is crucial not only from the point of view of minority rights in education, but also from the point of view of the pedagogical effectiveness of the entire teaching-learning process. At the same time, access to the language and culture of the majority is an important condition for the equal opportunities of pupils with minority affiliation. In order to foster the integration of minorities the multicultural content of mainstream education should be strengthened.

An inclusive environment that is provided by the schools, which are educating children belonging to minorities, should be strengthened. It refers to the relationship between teachers and students, teachers and parents and to the treatment of the children in schools.

In developing countries, governments strengthening minority involvement and building the capacity of minority organisations. Both grant-giving and operational programmes that address the problems of children with minority affiliation should have an inherent component of evaluation based on sound quality indicators.

Educational equity refers to an educational environment in which individuals can consider options and make choices based on their abilities and talents, not on the basis of stereotypes, biased expectations or discrimination. The achievement of educational equity enables females and males of all races and ethnic backgrounds develop skills needed to be productive, empowered citizens. It opens economic and social opportunities regardless of gender, ethnicity, race or social status.

Issues of Asian American Students

Asian Americans have had to fight a long battle to have access to desegregated and equal educational opportunities. In this historical context, some of the most important victories were the 1968 and 1969 student strikes at San Francisco State University and U.C. Berkeley that ultimately led to the establishment of the first Ethnic Studies and Asian American Studies programmes in the country. Since then, Asian Americans have faced many other issues when it comes to their educational experience. Perhaps the most far-reaching issue that Asian Americans still face is actually the most ironic.

In the past, Asian Americans were fighting mechanisms of prejudice, exclusion, and institutional discrimination that prevented them from even attending certain schools and therefore receiving a fair education. But recently, Asian Americans have been and continue to be touted as the one ethnic minority group that has successfully overcome racism and achieved the American dream, primarily through education. As the so-called "model minority", Asian Americans are frequently portrayed as a bright, shining example of hard work and patience whose example other minority groups should follow. Many people take these beliefs further and argue that since Asian Americans are doing so well, we no longer experience any discrimination and that Asian Americans no longer need services such as bilingual education, bilingual government documents, and public assistance.

About 42 per cent of all Asian American adults have at least a college degree, the highest of all the major racial/ethnic groups. It's also common for Asian American students to have the highest test scores and/or GPAs within any given high school or college cohort. But what usually gets left out is the fact that not all Asian Americans are the same. For every Chinese American or South Asian who has a college degree, the same number of South-east Asians are still struggling to adapt to their lives in the US.

The cultural stereotype that "all Asians are smart" puts a tremendous amount of pressure on many Asian Americans. Many, particularly Southeast Asians, are not able to conform to this unrealistic expectation and in fact, have the highest high school dropout rates in the country. Asian Americans who are struggling tend to be immigrants who have limited English proficiency. Many people don't know that more than half, 60 per cent in fact, of all Asian Americans are immigrants. Most are relatively fluent in English but a large portion are not. Therefore, similar to other immigrant minority groups, Asian Americans still have a need for bilingual education that is also culturally sensitive to their immigration experiences and family situations. For many of these recent Asian American immigrant families, the right to a formal education and all the trappings of school life for their children are very new concepts.

It is common for Asian American children to quickly assimilate their peers' norms about socialising, homework, growing sense of independence, and other activities surrounding school. This in turn can lead to conflict with their parents if the parents don't understand these activities and if they feel that their children are acculturating into "mainstream" American society too quickly and conversely, losing their traditional ethnic identity just as quickly. In times like these, knowledgeable educators and school administrators can play an important role in mediating these tensions before too much conflict arise that may lead the Asian American student to withdraw and possibly worse.

Another irony surrounding Asian Americans being labelled the "model minority" is that it can actually backfire to their detriment. Specifically, beginning in the 1980s, many more Asian Americans were applying to college than before. Soon, it became common for 10 per cent, 15 per cent, or more of a given university's student population to be of Asian ancestry at a time when Asians were only about 3 per cent of the general population. As a result, many universities actually became alarmed at the growing Asian American student population on their campuses, so much so that once the Asian proportion of their student population reached 10, 15 per cent, they began to reject Asian students who were clearly qualified.

Soon, Asian Americans were accusing universities such as U.C. Berkeley, UCLA, Stanford, Harvard, Princeton, and Brown of imposing a quota or upper limit on their admission numbers. After several protests and investigations, these universities admitted that there were problems with these admission procedures but never admitted any deliberate wrongdoing. Soon thereafter, many opponents of affirmative action began to argue that these Asian American students were "victims" of affirmative action, just like Whites. In other words, these Asian American students were being denied admission when other "less qualified" ethnic groups (implying Blacks, Latinos, and American Indians) were being admitted.

The real issue is not that Asian students are "competing" with other racial/ethnic minority groups. Rather, the real cause of this controversy is the widespread use of admissions factors that always seem to favor White applicants. These included "legacy clauses" in which the children of alumni are almost always admitted, regardless of their actual qualifications. Other factors that artificially lowered the admissions rates for Asian students included persistent stereotypes that Asian students were not "well-rounded" candidates and rarely participate in extracurricular activities. Again, national research showed that in terms of participating in sports, performing arts, academic and social clubs, and community activities, the rates for Asian students were almost identical to that of White students. The point is, contrary to the superficially rosy picture of Asian Americans as the "model minority" who have overcome racism and achieved universal educational success, in many respects, Asian Americans are still the targets of discrimination. In discussing these and other issues, Asian-Nation seeks to provide a concise but comprehensive exploration of the historical, political, economic, and cultural elements and issues that make up today's diverse Asian American community.

Initiatives to Enhance Intercultural Education

Since 1948, several international legal texts have been adopted which contain references to the promotion of intercultural education. For the most part, these texts belong to the category of human rights instruments that have been drafted within the framework of international organisations such as the United Nations, UNESCO and the Council of Europe. These texts are probably wellknown to human Rights lawyers. The public at large, professionals working in the field of (intercultural) education and politicians, however, tend not to be familiar with this kind of written legal material.

The basis for all international texts on education can be found in the Universal Declaration of Human Rights, which was adopted by the General Assembly of the United Nations on 10 December 1948. In principle this is a nonbinding instrument, but since its adoption it has gained wide approval and acceptance.

Article 26 of the Declaration deals with the right to education. Paragraph 2 stipulates the aims of education and reads: "Education shall be directed to the full development of the human personality and to the strengthening of respect for human rights and fundamental freedoms. It shall promote understanding, tolerance and friendship among all nations, racial or religious groups, and shall further the activities of the United Nations for the maintenance of peace." Some elements in this paragraph are important from the perspective of intercultural education. These are the full development of the human personality and the promotion of understanding, tolerance and friendship among people.

Since 1948, this clause has been cited and elaborated many times in other international human rights documents, such as treaties and recommendations. Some of these texts have a universal scope and were drafted within the framework of the United Nations or the UNESCO. Other texts have a regional character and were drafted within the framework of the Council of Europe and the Organisation of American States.

Article 7 of the International Convention on the Elimination of All Forms of Racial Discrimination deals with the important subject of combating the prejudices that lead to racial discrimination. According to this provision, States Parties undertake to adopt immediate and effective measures in the fields of teaching, education, culture and information to, *inter alia*, promote understanding, tolerance and friendship among nations and racial or ethnical groups.

Other universal texts, such as article 13, paragraph 1, of the International Covenant on Economic, Social and Cultural Rights and article 5 of the UNESCO Convention against Discrimination in Education correspond with the wording of article 26, paragraph 2, of the Universal Declaration. A more recent example is the Convention on the Rights of the Child. Article 29 of this Convention contains several new elements with regard to the cultural aspects of education that do not feature in the older texts.

Another recent instrument is the International Convention on the Protection of the Rights of All Migrant

Workers and Members of their Families. This convention contains a provision which focuses on the importance of education for the integration of migrant workers and their families in the states of employment. Special mention should also be made of the Declaration on the Rights of Persons Belonging to National or Ethnic, Religious and Linguistic Minorities. This Declaration was adopted by the General Assembly of the United Nations after many years of negotiations on a highly politically sensitive question such as the rights of minorities.

Article 4, paragraph 4, of this Declaration aims at promoting understanding between the minorities of a country and the other sections of the population through education. Lastly, the Declaration on the Elimination of All Forms of Intolerance and of Discrimination Based on Religion or Belief should be mentioned. In this instrument, it is stipulated that children should be brought up to respect freedom of religion or the beliefs of others, in full consciousness that their energy and talents should be devoted to serving their fellow humans. It is argued that this provision has a clear link to intercultural education.

In December 1994, the General Assembly of the United Nations adopted a resolution in which it proclaimed a United Nations Decade for Human Rights Education, beginning on 1 January 1995. This resolution contains a recommendation to governments, non-governmental educational agencies and governmental organisations to implement a Plan of Action that had been drawn up by the UN. In this resolution the General Assembly stressed that "human rights education should involve more than the provision of information and should constitute a comprehensive lifelong process by which people at all levels in development and in all strata of society learn respect for the dignity of others and the means and methods of ensuring respect in all societies". The objectives of the Decade for Human Rights Education have been formulated in the International Plan of Action in the following manner:

i) the assessment of needs and the formulation of effective strategies for the furtherance of human rights education at all school levels, in vocational training and formal as well as non-formal learning;

ii) the building and strengthening of programmes and capacities for human rights education at the international, regional, national and local levels;

iii) the coordinated development of human rights education materials;

iv) the strengthening of the role and capacity of the mass media in the furtherance of human rights education;

v) the global dissemination of the Universal Declaration of Human Rights in the maximum possible number of languages and in other forms appropriate for various levels of literacy and for the disabled.

This Plan of Action includes extensive and detailed recommendations, suggestions and guidelines for the implementation and promotion of human rights education, such as a recommendation to governments to draw up a national plan of action and a national committee for human rights education. It is also of interest for those in non-governmental organisations involved in the construction of teaching materials.

Several important texts on the promotion of intercultural education have been adopted within the framework of UNESCO. In 1974, the General Conference of UNESCO agreed upon a Recommendation concerning Education for International Understanding, Cooperation and Peace and Education relating to Human Rights and Fundamental Freedoms. Part III of this Recommendation starts with a reference to the aims of education as laid down in article 26, paragraph 2, of the Universal Declaration. It subsequently lists a number of guiding principles for educational policy. One of these principles is understanding and respect for all peoples, their cultures, civilisations, values and ways of life, including domestic ethnic cultures and cultures of other nations.

A link to intercultural education can also be found in paragraph 17, under which Member States of UNESCO should promote, at various stages and in various types of education, the study of different cultures, their reciprocal influences and their respective ways of life, in order to encourage mutual appreciation of the differences between them. In 1978, the General Conference of UNESCO adopted and solemnly proclaimed the Declaration on Race and Racial Prejudice. According to this Declaration, States have a responsibility to ensure that the educational resources of all countries are employed to combat racism. To this end, States should take all appropriate steps, including the drafting of legislation.

Another interesting text from the perspective of the promotion of intercultural education is the Declaration regarding Intolerance—a threat to democracy. On the basis of this Declaration, the Committee of Ministers decided "to promote an awareness of the requirements of human rights and the ensuing responsibilities in a democratic society, and to this end, in addition to human rights education, to encourage the creation in schools, from the primary level upwards, of a climate of active understanding of, and respect for, the qualities and cultures of others".

The promotion of intercultural education should not only take place in the curricula; a prerequisite is that teachers familiarise themselves and become experienced with the issue. In order to reach this goal, the Committee of Ministers adopted a recommendation on the training of teachers in education for intercultural understanding, particularly in a context of migration. The Committee recommended governments to make the intercultural dimension and the understanding between different communities a feature of initial and in-service teacher training.

In 1990s, the Council of Europe has devoted a great deal of attention to the situation and problems of national minorities in Europe. This was a reaction to the collapse of the communist systems in a number of Central and Eastern European countries and the ensuing emergence of claims for minority rights. As a result, governments of the member states of the Council of Europe agreed upon a treaty on the protection of national minorities: the Framework Convention for the Protection of National Minorities.

Article 6(1) stipulates that States shall encourage a spirit of tolerance and intercultural dialogue with a view to promoting mutual respect and understanding between all persons living in a country, so not only between members of different minorities. Article 12 specifies that the education system in a country may be an appropriate forum to contribute to the realisation of those goals.

Treaties are international agreements, concluded in written form between states, and governed by international law. Other designations for such agreements are, for example, "convention" or "covenant". States acting as subjects of international law can conclude treaties. It is, however, accepted that state members of a federal union may possess a certain capacity to conclude treaties if such a capacity is allowed by the federal constitution. In many states, treaties need to be approved by parliament and require ratification by the government before coming into effect in a particular state.

A treaty is binding for the contracting parties, who must perform it in good faith. This means that a treaty gives rise to legal obligations for states. When becoming a party to a treaty, a state must be sure that it is able and willing to comply with its provisions. Its national law, policy and practice must be in accordance with the letter and the spirit of the treaty. When a state wants to enact new legislation or makes a change in policy, the norms of a treaty must operate as a criterion. All agencies of a state must guarantee that they will act in accordance with the provisions of the treaty.

In most treaties that exist in the field of human rights, some kind of international supervisory procedure, such as a reporting procedure to an international body of experts, is provided for. Human rights treaties often afford states a certain discretion as to how to comply best with the norms. This does not mean, however, that treaties are permissive. On the contrary, the obligations still apply, but it is left to the individual state to choose the most appropriate means. In most cases, treaty provisions regarding intercultural education are not self-executing, but need to be implemented by the legislative and administrative authorities of a State Party.

The treaty provisions on intercultural education imply obligations for states to progressively realise the aims of such education. The character of the obligations, and the language used, imply that the addressee is the state, not the individual. These obligations cannot be invoked by individuals against the state. In legal terms, these provisions are not justiciable. States Parties, however, are obliged to guarantee that their national laws, policy and practice are in conformity with the relevant treaty provisions.

Non-governmental organisations focusing on intercultural education, as well as teachers, should promote knowledge of these international norms among the public at large, educational institutions, students, parents and politicians. Especially non-governmental organisations with expertise in this area must scrutinise the conduct of states, in particular when states report to international bodies on the progress made and the problems encountered in implementing international norms at a national level.

A system of shadow-reporting could be an effective means to that end. In conclusion, it can be stated that, although the legal character of the international documents on intercultural education is not as firm as people might wish and their implementation depends on governments' willingness to take measures, grassroots organisations can act as watch dogs, constantly reminding governments of the norms they have voluntarily endorsed.

Since the different nations of the world are interdependent, and since virtually all countries can be considered to be multicultural, the difference between international and intercultural understanding is not very relevant. In the different parts of the world different groups have different status, which causes inequality and discrimination. It is, therefore, not possible to deal with issues of diversity without dealing with issues of inequality. On the other hand, issues of inequality in a multicultural society cannot be addressed without dealing with cultural diversity.

Cultural diversity is not only caused by historical and contemporary migration, but also by individual differences between people, by differences in profession, religion, age, gender, abilities, education, and life experiences. Human rights are drafted to ensure that all people, wherever they are living, have the same rights as other people. Human rights are inclusive, i.e., there are no people who are excluded from human rights; human rights are aimed at the inclusion of all people in society. All people have the same rights to participate in the economic, social and cultural areas of society.

In the area of education, inclusiveness should be realised at the classroom level, which is the professional responsibility of the teacher, at the level of the school policy, which is the responsibility of the whole school community, particularly of the school management, and at the level of the educational system, which is materialised in educational legislation.

Intercultural and human rights education are also mainly focused on curriculum. However, measures in this area can only be effective if they include the organisation of the learning processes which take place in the school environment. Introducing human rights in the curriculum has consequences for the organisation of groups, classroom strategies and school climate.

Formal education systems are often rightly accused of stunting personal fulfilment by forcing all children into the same cultural and intellectual mould, without taking sufficient account of the variety of individual talents. They tend to emphasise, for example, the development of abstract knowledge to the detriment of other qualities such as imagination, the ability to communicate, leadership, a sense of beauty or the spiritual dimension of existence, or manual skills. Article 33 of the UNESCO recommendation of 1974 concerning education for international understanding, cooperation and peace and education relating to human rights and fundamental freedoms, and the Council of Europe Recommendation provide concrete criteria for intercultural teacher education.

Teachers are the professionals who convert policy guidelines for education into the organisation of learning processes. For this conversion of policy into the organisation of learning processes teachers need knowledge and skills. Equality of opportunities can only be achieved if children within the classroom have equal access to the learning process, which is managed by the teacher. Professional standards for teachers have to be derived from the criteria for education.

The aims of intercultural education can only be achieved through the organisation of interaction and communication. Management of learning processes implies the management of interaction processes in the classroom in such a way that all children participate.

References

Banks, J.A., "Multicultural Education for Freedom's Sake", *Educational Leadership, December/January,* pp. 32-36, 1992.

Hilliard, A.G., "Why We Must Pluralise the Curriculum", *Educational Leadership*, 49, pp. 12-14, 1992.

Ingram, Earl G., "A New Silence", *The Hispanic Outlook in Higher Education*, New Jersey, 2002.

Perez, Antonio, D. (ed.), "Hispanic Community Must Raise the Bar on Academic Achievement". *The Hispanic Outlook in Higher Education*, New Jersey, 2002.

Smitherman, Geneva (ed.), *Black English and the Education of Black Children and Youth: Proceedings of the National Invitational Symposium on the King Decision*, Detroit: Harlo Press, 1981.

Van Keulen, G., Weddington G., And DeBose C., Speech, Language, *Learning and the African-American Child,* Boston: Allyn Bacon, 1998.

Dyson, M. E., "Essentialism and the complexities of racial identity", In D. T. Goldberg (Ed.), *Multiculturalism: A critical reader*, Cambridge, MA: Blackwell Press, 2000.

Gay, G., "Curriculum theory and multicultural education", In J. A. Banks & C.A.M. Banks (eds.), *Handbook of research on multicultural education,* San Francisco: Jossey-Bass, 2001.

Glazer, N., *We are all multiculturalists now,* Cambridge, MA: Harvard University Press, 1997.

Grant, C. A., Sleeter, C. E., *Turning on learning: Five approaches for multicultural teaching plans for race, class, gender, and disability,* 2nd ed., Upper Saddle River, NJ: Merrill/ Prentice Hall, 1997.

Dei, George, "The Challenge of Anti-Racist Education in Canada" in *Canadian Ethnic Studies*, Volume 25, Issue 2, 1993.

Henson, K., *Curriculum Planning: Integrating Multiculturalism, Constructivism, and Educational Reform*, Boston: McGraw-Hill, 2001.

Ozmon, H and Craver, S., *Philosophical Foundations of Education*, Upper Saddle River: Prentice Hall, 1999.

Powell, R., Cantrell, S., Adams, S., "Saving Black Mountain: The Promise of Critical Literacy in a Multicultural Democracy" in *Reading Teacher*, Volume 54, Issue 8, May, 2001.

Sweeney, M., "No Easy Road to Freedom: Cultural Literacy in a Fourth Grade Classroom" in *Reading and Writing Quarterly*, Volume 13, Issue 3, July-September 1997.

Bibliography

Baca, L. M., Cervantes, H. T., *The bilingual special education interface*, Columbus, OH: Merill, 1989.

Baker, Colin, Sylvia Prys Jones, *Encyclopedia of Bilingualism and Bilingual Education*, Clevedon (Multilingual Matters), 1998

Banks, J. A. , *Educating Citizens in a Multicultural Society*, New York: Teachers College Press,1997.

_______________ , *Diversity within Unity: Essential Principles for Teaching and Learning in a Multicultural Society*, CME Publications, University of Washington, Seattle, 1995.

_______________ , "Multicultural Education for Freedom's Sake", *Educational Leadership, December / January,* pp. 32-36, 1992.

Baugh, I. W., Baugh, J. G., "Global classrooms: E-mail learning communities", *Learning and Leading with Technology*, 25 (3), 38-41, 1997.

Bennett, C., *Comprehensive multicultural education: Theory and Practice,* Massachusetts: Allen & Bacon, 1995.

_______________ , *Comprehensive multicultural education: Theory and practice,* Massachusetts: Allen & Bacon, 1995.

Bernard (ed.), *Concise Encyclopedia of Educational Linguistics*, London, Pergamon, 1999.

Byram, Michael (ed.), *Encyclopedia of Language Teaching and Learning*, London/New York, Routledge, 2000.

Carrasquillo, A. and Rodriguez, V., *Language minority students in the mainstream classroom*, England: Multilingual. Council for Exceptional Children, 1993.

_______________ , "Bilingual special education: The important connection", In A. Carrasquillo and R. Baecher (eds.), *Teaching the bilingual special education students,* NY: Ablex, 1990.

Castles, Stephen and Davidson, Alastair, *Citizenship and Migration: Globalisation and the Politics of Belonging*, New York: The Guilford Press, 2000.

Cortes, C. E., "Future will demand culturally literate citizens", *Thrust for Educational Leadership*, 7(3), 20-22, 1978,

Cummins, J., *Bilingualism and special education: Issues in assessment and pedagogy*, San Diego, CA: College-Hill, 1984.

_____________ , Sayers, D., "Multicultural Education and Technology", *Multicultural Education*, 3(3), 4-11, 1996.

Cummins, Jim, David Corson (eds.), *Bilingual Education*, 1997.

Damarin, S. K., "Technology and multicultural education: The question of convergence", *Theory Into Practice*, 37(1), 11-19, 1998.

Dandy, Evelyn B., *Black Communications: Breaking Down the Barriers*, Chicago: African American Images, 1991.

Davis, King, "Race, Health Status, and Managed Care", in Epstein, Len and Brisbane, Francis (eds.), *Cultural Competence Series*, Rockville, MD: Center for Substance Abuse Prevention, 1997.

Dei, George, "The Challenge of Anti-Racist Education in Canada" in *Canadian Ethnic Studies*, Volume 25, Issue 2, 1993.

Delpit, Lisa and Dowdy, Jo Ann (eds.), *The Skin We Speak: Thoughts on Language and Culture in the Classroom*, New York: New Press, 2002.

DeVoogd, G. L., "Computer use levers power sharing: Multicultural students' styles of participation and knowledge", *Computers & Education*, 31(4), 351-364, 1998.

Dimidjian, V.J., "Holiday, Holy Days, and Wholly Dazed", *Young Children*, 1989.

Diversity and Citizenship Education: Global Perspectives, San Francisco: Jossey-Bass, 2003.

Dixon, G.T., Fraser, S., "Teaching Preschoolers in a Multilingual Classroom", *Childhood Education*, 1986.

Donovan, M. Suzanne and Cross, Christopher T., *Minority Students in Special and Gifted Education, Commission on Minority Representation in Special and Gifted Education, Behavioural and Social Sciences and Education,* National Research Council, Washington, DC: National Academy Press, 2001.

Dyson, M. E., "Essentialism and the complexities of racial identity", In D. T. Goldberg (Ed.), *Multiculturalism: A critical reader*, Cambridge, MA: Blackwell Press, 2000.

Education in the 80s: Multiethnic education, Washington, D.C.: National Education Association, 1981

Extra Guus, Yagmur Kutlay, *Language diversity in multicultural Europe*, Paris: UNESCO, 2002.

Freedman, K., Liu, M., "The importance of computer experience, learning processes, and communication patterns in multicultural networking", *Educational Technology Research and Development*, 44(1), 43-59, 1996.

Gay, G., "Curriculum for multicultural education", In F. H. Klassen and D. M. Gollnick (eds.), *Pluralism and the American teacher: Issues and Case Studies,* Washington, DC: American Association of Colleges for Teacher Education, 1977.

______________ , "Curriculum theory and multicultural education", In J. A. Banks & C.A.M. Banks (eds.), *Handbook of research on multicultural education,* San Francisco: Jossey-Bass, 2001.

Glazer, N., *We Are All Multiculturalists Now*, Cambridge, MA: Harvard University Press, 1997.

Gloria Ladson Billings, *New Directions in Multicultural Education: Complexities, Boundaries, and Critical Race Theory,* University of Wisconsin, Madison.

Gollnick, D. M., Chinn, P. C., *Multicultural Education in a Pluralistic Society,* St. Louis: Mosby, 1990.

Gordon, B. M., "Knowledge Construction, Competing Critical Theories, and Education", In *Handbook of Research on Multicultural Education,* J. A. Banks and C. A. McGee Banks (eds.), New York: Macmillan, 1995

Grant, C. A., Sleeter, C. E., *Turning on learning: Five approaches for multicultural teaching plans for race, class, gender, and disability,* 2nd ed., Upper Saddle River, NJ: Merrill/ Prentice Hall, 1997.

Hakuta, K., Garcia, E., "Bilingualism and Education", *American Psychologist*, 1989.

Hamayan, E. V., Kwiat, J. A., and Perlman, R., *Assessment of language minority students: A handbook for educators*, Chicago: Illinois Resource Centre, 1985.

Hehir, Thomas and Latus, Thomas, "Special Education at Century's End: Evaluation of Theory and Practice Since 1970", *Harvard Educational Review Reprint Series,* Number 23,1992 .

Heller, Kirby A., Holtzman, Wayne H., and Messick, Samuel (eds.), *Placing Children in Special Education: A Strategy for Equity,* Washington, DC: National Academy Press, 1982.

Henson, K., *Curriculum Planning: Integrating Multiculturalism, Constructivism, and Educational Reform*, Boston: McGraw-Hill, 2001.

Hilliard, A.G., "Why We Must Pluralise the Curriculum", *Educational Leadership*, 49, pp. 12-14, 1992.

Hinnenkamp, Volker, "Constructing Misunderstanding as a Cultural Event" In: A. di Luzio, S. Günthner & F. Orletti (eds.), *Culture in Communication. Analyses of intercultural situations*, Amsterdam / Philadelphia: J. Benjamins, 2001.

Hoff, Gerd, "Multicultural Education in Germany: Historical Development and Current Status", In J. A. Banks & C. A. M. Banks (eds.), *Handbook of Research on Multicultural Education*, New York: MacMillan, 1995.

Ichilov, Orit (ed.), *Citizenship and Citizenship Education in a Changing World*, London: The Woburn Press, 1998.

Ingram, Earl G., "A New Silence", *The Hispanic Outlook in Higher Education*, New Jersey, 2002.

Irvine, J. J., and York, D. E., "Learning Styles and Culturally Diverse Students". In *Handbook of Research on Multicultural Education*, edited by J. A. Banks and C. A. McGee Banks, New York: Macmillan, 1995.

Kagan, S.L., Garcia, E.E., "Educating Culturally and Linguistically Diverse Preschoolers: Moving the Agenda", *Early Childhood Research Quarterly*, 1991.

King, J. E., "Culture-centered knowledge: Black studies, curriculum transformation, and social action", In J. A. Banks, C.A.M. Banks Eds., *Handbook of research on multicultural education*, San Francisco: Jossey-Bass, 2001.

Klassen, F. H., and D. M. Gollnick (eds.), *Pluralism and the American teacher: Issues and Case Studies,* Washington, DC: American Association of Colleges for Teacher Education, 1977.

Kozol, Jonathan Savage, *Inequalities: Children in America's Schools*, New York: Crown, 1991.

Kymlicka, W., (ed.), *The Rights of Minority Cultures,* New York: Oxford University Press, 1995.

Kymlicka, Will Multicultural Citizenship: A Liberal Theory of Minority Rights, New York: Oxford University Press, 1995.

Ladson-Billings, G, "Just what is critical race theory and what's it doing in a nice field like education?" *International Journal of Qualitative Studies in Education,* 1998.

Lee, C. C. (ed.), *Counseling for diversity: A guide for school counselors and related professionals,* Boston, MA: Allyn & Bacon, 1995.

Lidz, Carol and Elliott, Julian G. (eds.), *Dynamic Assessment: Theory, Models, and Applications*, New York: Pantheon Books, 2000.

Luchtenberg, Sigrid (ed.), *Migration, Education and Change*, London: Routledge, 2003.

Lynch, James, *Education for Citizenship in a multicultural society*, London/New York, Cassell, 1992.

Martin Puetz (ed.), *Language Choices. Conditions, constraints, and consequences*, Amsterdam/Philadelphia, John Benjamins Publishing Company, 1997.

Nieto, S., "School reform and student Achievement: A multicultural perspective", in J. A. Banks, C. A. M. Banks (eds.), *Multicultural Education: Issues and Perspectives,* Boston: Allyn and Bacon, 1997.

Norton, D.E., "Language and Cognitive Development Through Multicultural Literature", *Childhood Education*, 1985.

Olneck, M., "The recurring dream: Symbolism and ideology in intercultural and multicultural education", *American Journal of Education,* 98(2), 147–174, 1990.

Omizo, M. M., and D'Andrea, M. J., "Multicultural classroom guidance", In C. C. Lee (ed.), *Counseling for diversity: A guide for school counselors and related professionals,* Boston, MA: Allyn & Bacon, 1995.

Ozmon, H and Craver, S., *Philosophical Foundations of Education*, Upper Saddle River: Prentice Hall, 1999.

Parker, W. C., *Teaching Democracy: Unity and Diversity in Public Life*, New York: Teachers College Press, 2003.

Pederson, P. and J. C. Carey (eds.), *Multicultural Counseling in Schools: A Practical Handbook,* Boston, MA: Allyn & Bacon, 1994.

Perez, Antonio, D. (ed.), "Hispanic Community Must Raise the Bar on Academic Achievement". *The Hispanic Outlook in Higher Education*, New Jersey, 2002.

Phillips, C.B., "Nurturing Diversity For Today's Children and Tomorrow's Leaders", *Young Children*, 1988.

Powell, R., Cantrell, S., Adams, S., "Saving Black Mountain: The Promise of Critical Literacy in a Multicultural Democracy" in *Reading Teacher*, Volume 54, Issue 8, May, 2001.

Ramirez, J.D., & Douglas, D., *Language minority parents and the school: Bridging the gap*, Sacramento: California State Dept. of Education, Office of Bilingual Bicultural Education.

Ramirez, M. and Castaneda, A., *Cultural Democracy, Bicognitive Development and Education*, New York: Academic Press, 1974.

Ravitch, D., "Multiculturalism: E-pluribus plures", *American Scholar*, 59(3), 337–354, 1990.

Roblyer, M.D., Dozier-Henry, O., Burnette, A. P., "Technology and multicultural education: The uneasy alliance", *Educational Technology*, 36(5), 5-12, 1996.

Sleeter, C. E. , *Multicultural Education as Social Activism*, Albany: State University of New York Press, 1997.

Smitherman, Geneva (ed.), *Black English and the Education of Black Children and Youth: Proceedings of the National Invitational Symposium on the King Decision*, Detroit: Harlo Press, 1981.

Sweeney, M., "No Easy Road to Freedom: Cultural Literacy in a Fourth Grade Classroom" in *Reading and Writing Quarterly*, Volume 13, Issue 3, July-September 1997.

Trueba, H. T., "*Success or failure? Learning and the language minority students*", Rowley, MA: Newbury, 1987.

Van Keulen, G., Weddington G., And DeBose C., Speech, Language, *Learning and the African-American Child,* Boston: Allyn Bacon, 1998.

Watts and Jerzy J. Smolicz (eds.), *Cultural Democracy and Ethnic Pluralism, Multicultural and multilingual Policies in Education*, Bern et al.: Peter Lang Verlag, 125-148, 1997.

Willett, C. (ed.), *Theorising Multiculturalism: A Guide to the Current Debate*, Malden, MA: Blackwell, 1998.

Wittrock, M. C., "Constructing useful theories of teaching English from recent research in the cognitive process of language", In J. Squire (ed.), *The dynamics of language*, Urbana, Ill: Clearinghouse in Reading and Communication Skills, 1987.

Wodak, Ruth, David Corson (eds.), *Language Policy and Political Issues in Education*, 1997.

Index